White Magic
and
English Renaissance Drama

White Magic
and
English Renaissance
Drama

David Woodman

Rutherford • *Madison* • *Teaneck*
Fairleigh Dickinson University Press

© 1973 by Associated University Presses, Inc.

Associated University Presses, Inc.
Cranbury, New Jersey 08512

Library of Congress Cataloging in Publication Data

Woodman, David, 1925–
    White magic and English Renaissance drama.

    Bibliography: p.
    1. English drama—Early modern and Elizabethan—History
and criticism. 2. Magic in literature. 3. Magic—History. I. Title.
PR658.M27W65   822′.3′0937   72-423
ISBN 0-8386-1125-7

Printed in the United States of America

To my mother and father

Contents

Acknowledgments

I wish to acknowledge all those who have made this book possible. In particular, I should like to single out Professor S. F. Johnson of Columbia University, Christopher Mulvey, John Young, Sidney Hollister, and Ardelle Striker.

Introduction

A theatergoer in the late English Renaissance was offered in the plays that he saw two contrasting views of the universe. The medieval Ptolemaic concept of the universe was that of a divine unity to the endless diversification of nature, a unity culminating in a vast network of correspondences that harmoniously connected man as a microcosm to God and the cosmos. Alternatively, a new attitude, taking hold during the early decades of the seventeenth century, posed that such closely knit interrelationships did not exist. The universe, instead, consisted of parts integrated in growth, yet isolated, thus leaving man with a sense of nature's detachment and indifference. Until the advent of this empirical view, however, the majority of thinking men believed themselves to be an integrated part of the transcendent unity of man, nature, and God.

In essence, white magic reflects this theory of unity, for the white magician assumes that God has concealed within the framework of the universe specific divine powers or virtues available to him through ritual and meditation. Attracting such powers through the celestial aid of angels, spirits, stars, and planets, or through invoking the terrestrial virtues of the four elements, or those of animals, plants, metals, and stones, the magician channels these sources of

11

divine energy through himself to affect the harmonious outcome of his beneficent works. Like the king who as God's
deputy also possesses divine powers, the white magician
heals those who seek his aid and imposes benevolent order
on anarchy.

Since we are primarily concerned here with the treatment
of white magic in English Renaissance drama and the likely
responses of then-contemporary audiences to magic, this
study will explore some of the sources and history of white
magic and relate them to sixteenth- and seventeenth-century
English culture. Many works examine Renaissance magic,
both black and white, and although this investigation relies
on some of these, its purpose is rather to gain insight into
an aspect of Renaissance life familiar to some Elizabethans
but unfamiliar to the modern reader.[1] The more sensational
acts of black magicians have received greater attention, yet
several playwrights introduce white magic, on one level as
a device for plot manipulation, on a deeper level, as a symbolic force for good, and often as a butt for satire. Each
of these aspects of the Elizabethan and Jacobean stage
deserves close scrutiny, particularly in the case of such
masterpieces as *The Tempest* and *The Alchemist*. Before
embarking upon such an exploration, however, we should
first consider how the white magician relates to his most
typical activities, how the sources of white magic became
unified into one concept, how Elizabethan audiences must
have recognized and responded to white magic, and how
particular forces stimulated a popular belief in magic.

The white magician can receive and transmit the sources
of divine power only through supreme dedication and study
and by undertaking acts of self-purification that prepare
him to be the suitable agent of God. Having endeavored
to perfect himself through eradicating base elements from

---

1. Both R. H. West's study of pneumatology in Elizabethan drama in *The
Invisible World* (Athens, Ga., 1939) and Robert H. Reed Jr.'s, *The Occult
on the Tudor and Stuart Stage* (Boston, 1965), are guides in relating
magic to drama.

his own character, he can then strive to raise all that is inferior to a state of perfection. A clear demonstration of this is alchemy, in which the magician uses fire to remove the baseness of the inferior metals of lead, iron, copper, tin, and mercury, thereby transmitting them into their perfect essence—gold and silver.

Besides alchemy, the three other major areas of the white magician's work include natural astrology, the raising of Neoplatonic daemons, and healing with herbs. As astrologist, he believes the planets and stars possess both life and intelligence, endowed with divine powers by God, the Prime Mover. Thus, he times his magic to coincide with that particular character of each planet whose special influence changes sublunary events and affects the hidden virtues of plants, animals, and minerals.[2] In such a universal scheme, each terrestrial natural object is subject to its own planetary influence and possesses an individual sympathetic virtue in accordance with that influence.

As a summoner of beneficial spirits, he calls upon Neoplatonic daemons to be agents between himself and God, eliciting from them divine powers and messages that he could not otherwise intercept. Such "middle spirits"[3] inhabit a neutral space between earth and the aether enveloping the moon. Belonging in both air and aether, with bodies less substantial than clouds, they are usually invisible to man. Their function, in accord with the Principle of Plenitude through which all regions are inhabited, is to sustain a harmonious design between beings in the aether and on

---

2. Natural astrology, the province of the white magician, a matter of timing the propitious influences of planets with the divine natural virtues of plants, animals, and minerals, must not be confused with judicial astrology. The latter focuses on the prognostication of events through the influence of the stars, a form of predestination that disallowed man the use of his will. Both Catholics and Protestants inveighed against such divination, but natural astrology, not claiming foresight, gained some approval, from figures such as Francis Bacon and King James I, who at the same time denounced judicial astrology.

3. John Milton, *Paradise Lost,* III, 461, in *Complete Poems and Major Prose,* ed. Merritt Y. Hughes (New York, 1957).

Earth, acting as a third force to link man with God.[4] Obviously they are not to be mistaken for devils or demons, those rebellious spirits of Satan or Lucifer whom God expelled from Heaven, and whom the black magician invokes for his temporal, personal gratification. Finally, as healer, the white magician extracts specific divine virtues from plants, minerals, and animals—all of which are individually influenced by planets—and with them concocts his curative medicines.

Since white magic was essentially a hybrid, it drew upon a wide variety of occult traditions for its content, at one point borrowing from Hermetism or the cabala, at another taking something from Pythagoreanism. Eventually these three areas of occult practice came together in Neoplatonism, reemerging within their new framework as overlapping but recognizably separate subdivisions of white magic: *divine magic,* which was dependent on God's personal revelation, achieved through invocation, the cabala, Hermetism, and the use of Neoplatonic daemons;[5] *natural magic,* primarily alchemy, which explored the sympathetic virtues and properties that could be discovered in tangible things, especially in metals; and *celestial magic,* which based itself essentially on astrology and used mathematics, Hermetism, and the cabala. Practitioners of all three kinds of magic, and white magicians in general, zealously restricted their knowledge to the eyes and ears of a coterie of initiates, thereby protecting their secrets against any outside abuse. Writings that did exist showed "only the crust of the mysteries to the vulgar, while reserving the marrow of the true sense

---

4. See C. S. Lewis, *The Discarded Image* (Cambridge, 1964), pp. 49–60. Lewis cites Plato (*Timaeus* [31^b-c]) and states that there must always exist a third force to bind two forces together, and it is daemons that act as this bridge linking man and the gods. Chalcidius, who is believed to have lived in the fourth century, translated segments of the *Timaeus*. To the scholars of the Middle Ages, this work became more representative of Plato than any other.
5. *Ibid.*

for higher and more perfected spirits,"[6] spirits who could also comprehend the magical arcana submerged within the texts of Orphic hymns, Hermetism, the cabala, and the Bible.

When Moses received from God a written law for the guidance of mankind, he shared his secrets with only seventy elders, thus creating the cabalistic tradition of orally transmitting this kind of secret knowledge from generation to generation. At the same time, God endowed him with special knowledge for invoking a hierarchy of angels to aid his spiritual leadership. A further aid to Moses was the doctrine of *sephiroth*, a two-way path between man and God through which God manifested himself. A series of ten emanations on different levels of descent brought God in touch with man's world.[7]

Three manipulative exegetic processes were described in the cabala as ways to uncover hidden meanings in the Scripture: *gemetria* worked with numbers, *notarikon* with letters, and *themurah* with words. By using this cryptic system and the *sephiroth*, or root of all roots, the cabalist sought to master the multiple meaning scriptural words had for God.[8] If successful, he would reach God's intellectual world. The cabala, however, was not a rigid method of mystical and theosophical thought. White magicians, for example, used manipulative cabalistic techniques in trying to harness nature. Concealed within the various combinations of letters that spelled out the divine names of God were, the magicians believed, the miraculous powers that contained the energy they needed. Moreover, since the cabala was theurgic in concept and dependent upon initiation rites to transmit the names of God from master to student, it naturally appealed to the white magician.

6. Pico, *Commento*, III, xi, 9, quoted in Edgar Wind, *Pagan Mysteries in the Renaissance* (New Haven, 1938), p. 24.
7. Joseph Leon Blau, *The Christian Interpretation of the Cabala in the Renaissance* (New York, 1944), p. 46.
8. *Ibid.,* pp. 8-9.

Many early Renaissance figures took a serious interest in cabalistic processes, two noteworthy instances being Pico della Mirandola (1463-1494) and Johann Reuchlin (1455-1522). Pico was responsible for Christianizing the cabala, for he substituted and justified Christian concepts within its scheme and employed them in scriptural interpretation. At a time when previous systems were also investigated in the hope of producing suggestive parallels, Reuchlin found congruencies between the cabala and Pythagoreanism. Given a basic concept that held the relationships of numbers as the essences of all things, it was practically inevitable that Pythagoreanism would become as vital to white magic as the cabala. As the correspondences of the Great Chain of Being of the Middle Ages were often symbolically related through numbers, so the earliest systems of numbers in Babylonia were linked tó astrological readings. What is more, the Israelites absorbed these Babylonian systems into the Old Testament, aided by the fact that ancient Hebraic writing stressed the sameness of items that were identified by similar numbers.[9] With these recognizable identities, which were the core of astrology, prophecy became feasible.

Growing independently from Babylonian and Hebrew influences, the Greek numerical system also stressed unity in an ordered universe. Its creator, Pythagoras (*c*. 580-*c*. 500 B.C.), emigrated to southern Italy after much travel and founded an isolated secret cult that believed in a numerical formulation of all things in the universe. Chronicling Pythagorean theories that linked the structure of numbers to that of music, Aristotle declared at a later time that

> the modifications and ratios of the musical scales were expressible in numbers;—since then all other things seemed in their whole nature to be modelled on numbers, and numbers seemed to be the first things in the whole of nature they supposed the elements of

9. Vincent Paul Hopper, *Medieval Number Symbolism* (New York, 1938), pp. 23-25.

number to be the elements of all things, and the whole heaven to be a musical scale and a number. And all the properties of numbers and scales which they could show to agree with the attributes and parts and the whole arrangement of the heavens, they collected and fitted into their scheme; and if there was a gap anywhere, they readily made additions so as to make their whole theory coherent.[10]

Crucial to this scheme was the decad, a series of one to ten that covered all possible combinations and became the basic concept for a cosmic theory. To it was added the principles of geometric form, thus providing Pythagoreans with an additional bridge between the abstractions of numerology and concrete reality.[11] With its emphasis on limit and unity, Pythagoreanism reinforced the belief that fundamental truth was identifiable in numbers and lent considerable support to the carefully ordered image of the medieval universe, where each man was a microcosm linked to God and the cosmos.

The notion of many connected to the oneness of God was also an essential part of the writings of the fictitious Hermes Trismegistus in the *Corpus Hermeticum*. As a work that disclosed infinite possibilities open to the man who probed the mysteries of nature, it revealed many rituals by which he might attract divine powers through image making:

(Hermes) . . . Our first ancestors . . . invented the art of making gods. . . . they added a virtue appropriate to it, taken from the world's nature, and mixed these; since they could not make souls, they evoked the souls of demons and angels, and put them into images with holy and divine rites, so that through these souls the idols might have the power of doing good and evil. . . . (Asclepius) . . . of what kind is the quality of these terrestrial gods? (Hermes) It consists, O Asclepius, of herbs, stones, and aromas, which have in them a natural divine power. And it is for the following reason the people delight them with frequent sacri-

---

10. Aristotle, *Metaphysica*, trans. W. D. Ross (Oxford, 1908), a, 5.
11. Rudolph Koch's *The Book of Signs*, trans. Vyvyan (London, 1930), contains descriptions of such geometric forms as well as magical signs.

fices, with hymns and praises and sweet sounds concerted like the harmony of the heavens: that this heavenly thing, which has been attracted into the idol by repeated heavenly rites, may bear joyously with men and stay with them long.[12]

Since these ceremonies induced divine powers into idols through the medium of a daemon's or angel's soul, it opened up a Pandora's box of pagan idol worship and made it almost impossible to defend the use of magic in a Christian setting. In general, the *Corpus* consisted of a collection of semipagan, mystical revelations overlaid with Stoicism. Some of the revelations included magical concepts that relied heavily on Platonism; others contained a variety of Jewish and Persian insights into magic.

Renaissance philosophers of white magic held varied attitudes toward Hermetism; some found it safer to ignore it, while others adopted its pagan aspects.[13] Ficino,[14] who translated a small portion of the *Corpus* into Greek in 1460, personally believed Hermes to be a contemporary of Moses and the work described to be that of early Greek philosophers. The theory grew that rites for white magic had developed many centuries before in Egypt, the country where all aspects of knowledge were thought to have originated. To an era dedicated to the works of antiquity, the theory had great appeal. It seemed possible to some that even Plato himself was indebted to Hermes. In addition, *Asclepius,* which came to light because of the *Corpus,* was thought to prophesy the coming of the Son of God, an attribution that certainly enhanced the spiritual authority of all the Hermetic writings.

Although this theory survived for approximately one

---

12. Asclepius, c. xiii, *Corpus Hermeticum,* ed. A. D. Nock and A. J. Festugiere (Paris, 1945), pp. 347–49, quoted in D. P. Walker, *Spiritual Magic from Ficino to Campanella* (London, 1958), pp. 40–41.

13. See Frances Yates, *Giordano Bruno and the Hermetic Tradition* (London, 1964). The writer is indebted to Miss Yates's masterly investigation of the Hermetic tradition.

14. See Paul O. Kristeller, *The Philosophy of Marsilio Ficino,* trans. Virginia Conant (Gloucester, Mass., 1964).

hundred and fifty years, the *Corpus* actually was compiled about two or three centuries after Christ. After Isaac Casaubon fixed this date in 1614, an alliance between these writings and the Scriptures was no longer feasible. "Hermes Trismegistus" turned out to be a fictitious creation, the assembled work of several authors, obviously unavailable to Plato.

Until this discovery, however, the man who sought divine power might well have drawn upon Hermetism. Originally, there were supposed to have been forty-two books, some of which were guides to training for priests, and to those prayers, processions, and sacrifices appropriate to worship at Egyptian festivals. Other books explored medicine, astronomy, and astrology, as well as laws and special rules for the king. By the fifteenth century, most of the books no longer existed.

Ficino, in fact, translated only four treatises.[15] The first, the *Pimander,* investigated the creation of the world; another, the *Asclepius,* enumerated specific Egyptian religious rites. Both claimed that the soul attained revelation through communion with divine power. To the skilled student of Hermes, all terrestrial materials possessed occult virtues infused with powers by their appropriate planets. His major task was to gain a familiarity with those particular animals, stones, and metals under the sign of each planet, and combine this knowledge with the best astrological timing. Only then might he expect his idols to absorb and reflect magical powers.

The last pagan figures whose philosophy combined supernatural and ascetic goals were Plotinus, Porphyry, Iamblichus, and Proclus. Their mystical otherworldliness bore certain similarities to that of the Christian Fathers, who were their contemporaries and who also claimed to have visions. As had to happen, the Church eventually disowned the pagans, banning what remained of their worship in A.D. 390. Yet, since pagans and Christians had often unwittingly

---

15. Yates, p. 27.

imitated and influenced each other, the Church had actually absorbed and syncretized many pagan tenets. In a quandary over where to draw the line between what it had already assimilated of ancient philosophy and what still remained outside its pale, the Church tended toward a policy of exclusion, finally ruling out the residuum of those philosophies —including white magic.

White Magic
and
English Renaissance Drama

1

White Magic and the Church

*T*hose Renaissance philosophers who counted white magic among their varied pursuits held a tenuous relationship with both Church and society over this particular vocation. On the one hand they might be privately fascinated with magic, while on the other, they sometimes publicly disclaimed any personal interest in it. This denial acted as a form of self-protection from the rebukes of the Church and also served to dissociate the philosophers from charlatan practitioners. The attitudes of the Church as well as the ideas of such philosophers as Ficino, Pico, Bruno, and Della Porta in Italy, and Agrippa and Dee[1] in northern Europe reflect some of the contemporary thinking prevalent in Renaissance society.

The most popular beliefs about magic of all kinds emanated from the Church. Augustine, one of its earliest spokesmen on the subject, condemned all magic as sleight of

---

1. Marsilio Ficino (1433–1499), Pico della Mirandola (1463–1494), Giordano Bruno (1548–1600), Giambattista Della Porta (c. 1538–1615), Henrich Cornelius Agrippa von Nettesheim (1486–1535), and John Dee (1527–1608).

hand intended to delude men. To him, there could be no comparison between such powers and the divine miracles of Christ, whose wonder-working did not call upon "incantations and charms composed under the influence of a criminal tampering with the unseen world." This was the province of magicians, opponents of one God and "the slaves of the deceitful rites of the demons whom they invoke under the names of angels."[2] Punishable with eternal damnation, the magician was a feigner and an imposter; his work was criticized as presumptuous and pagan, a stigma that the Renaissance white magician inherited.

Early Christian leaders particularly condemned judicial astrology: a reverence for planets and the forecasting of events that posed a threat to all Christian doctrines of free will. Churchmen built their case upon the supremacy of the spirit and faith in God versus the temporal quest for knowledge *(curiositas)*. St. Paul had warned men not to heed the philosophy and "vain deceit" of others.[3] The judicial astrologer, therefore, received the strongest criticism in the Renaissance; for example, in 1604 Thomas Wright complained, "What vain studies, exercise (for the most part) our Judiciarie Astronomers, by calculating nativities, foretelling events, prescribing the limits of men's lives, foreshewing their perille and dangers, by meer cosinage, and vaine curiosity?"[4] Judicial astrology, it was asserted, opened the door to personal pride, heresy, and an abandonment of faith. Its claims to prediction jeopardized the concept of free will, for, deprived of this, man had no need to depend on God.[5]

As natural astrologer, however, the white magician aus-

---

2. Augustine, *The City of God,* trans. Marcus Dods, X, 9 (New York, 1950), p. 312.
3. Colossians 2:8.
4. Thomas Wright, *The Passions of the Mind* (London, 1604), p. 315.
5. See Hardin Craig, *The Enchanted Glass* (Oxford, 1960), p. 267; for works on astrology, see also E. A. Strathmann, *Sir Walter Ralegh* (New York, 1951), pp. 172–96.

piciously timed influences of planets to affect the special natural energies of such sublunary things as plants, animals, and minerals, and thereby brought about his beneficent magic. He was a miracle worker, but he did not incur the charge of fatalism.[6]

A further deterrent to the white magician was the Protestant Reformation's denunciation of all miracles. Calvin, and to a lesser extent Luther, advanced the belief that miracles had not been necessary since the time of Christ and his disciples. All lives were predestined, Calvinism claimed, and miracles were the work of the Devil; moreover, astrological law and white magic, not being clearly found in Scripture, were regarded with deep suspicion as a pagan influence, dangerous to salvation. Apart from Christ, Calvinism denied intermediary beings between man and God, naturally striking at the white magician's use of daemons. The earlier image that daemons were good, fostered by the white magician, was rejected. In the light of such attitudes it is not surprising that the Reformation launched an intensified attack on all witchcraft.

Like other forms of white magic, alchemy was also subject to the Church's denunciation. As early as 1317, a papal decree threatened to punish alchemists with forfeit of any manufactured gains, and if the culprit were a cleric, with the removal of his benefices. In addition, excommunication was the lot of friars who did not burn all their books on alchemy.

Although the pursuit of alchemy was more easily defended than that of astrology, the creator of gold was believed to be tampering with God's design of the universe. It was feared, moreover, that alchemical rituals were drawn from black magic. William Perkins, a skeptic of alchemy, declared that "the Alchymist is to be reproved, that spends his time, and substance in labouring to change baser mettals

---

6. See D. C. Allen, *The Star-Crossed Renaissance* (Durham, N. C., 1941), and Johnstone Parr, *Tamburlaine's Malady* (University of Alabama, 1953).

into gold, a thing in truth impossible."[7] Yet, despite acts promising severe punishment for the practice of alchemy, the effect of Church and State prohibitions was not absolute.

A more practical impediment to the practice of alchemy, and one that directly stimulated charlatanism, was its need for considerable financial underwriting. Indeed, alchemical discovery could not have gone on throughout the Renaissance without the lure of incredible riches to entice men of means and heads of state to support it. The veil of secrecy that masked the alchemist's activities, combined with the protective obscurity of his writings, made it impossible to discern who was attempting a genuine transmutation and who was masquerading, extorting money, and devising means to arouse the hopes of his current guarantor.[8]

To be sure, the Church did not forbid all scientific inquiry, but it did insist that undue endeavors revealed a dissatisfaction with what God had provided; man was overreaching his province in uncovering God's secrets. And if the goal of the magician was fame alone, he would also be criticized, for fame was an object of desire constantly under attack by medieval churchmen, who spoke against temporal gain and advocated contemplation. It was possible, moreover, that the Devil pretended to impart accurate information about the universal laws of God; whatever the Devil shared would inevitably lure the victim from his faith in God.

Magicians refuted these allegations, claiming their investigations to be solely concerned with white magic, which had nothing to do with the Devil. Rather, their magic could only draw them closer to God, without whom, they declared, their operations would be impossible. This claim allowed the debate to center upon establishing the limits of white magic and its tangency with the supernatural. Reasoning from a Neoplatonic viewpoint, the magicians asserted that the

---

7. William Perkins, "A Treatise of Callings," in *Works* (1605), p. 920.
8. See below, chap. 6.

planets themselves had received occult energies from God. The Church, however, would not recognize the claim that matter could conceal energies and properties within it. Even so broad a churchman as Hooker, who structured codes in the *Laws of Ecclesiastical Polity,* cautioned his reader against presumptuously expecting to understand all natural laws. The familiar message of most Churchmen was for man to pay heed to his soul and avoid overreaching. A number of them, however, singled out magicians for a stronger attack, putting immense effort into confining their activities and branding them as atheists.

Although white magic occasionally had support from influential laymen such as Francis Bacon, many secular authorities were as vehemently against magic, white or black, as the churchmen. Jean Bodin, though astute in assessing contemporary political theory, censured all magic as black and refused to accept alternative views. For example, in his *De le Demonamie des Sorciers,* he asserted that demons flew through the air and men could be changed into animals.[9] King James VI of Scotland in his *Daemonologie* drew no distinction among magicians, mentioning the familiar problem of *Curiositas* in astrology while adding that the need for demons to support such wonders was evidence of black magic.[10] In this work, which he published before acceding to the English throne, James inveighed against magic and endorsed the death penalty indiscriminately for witches, magicians, or their customers. He also believed in many of the commonplace superstitions of the time, e.g., that witches could not shed tears and that their bodies would float on water and were marked with sores by the Devil, who transported them through the air. Not surprisingly, in 1604 James reaffirmed a statute against witchcraft and the conjuration of demons that had originally been passed in 1563.

In this excitable climate of Church and secular opposition

9. 1580, chap. 3, p. 19v.
10. 1597, p. 10.

to his activities, the benevolent magus was forced to admit that some of his procedures were also used by black magicians. Included were the operation of physical objects through names and numbers, the setting up of metal seals in order to receive occult energies from the planets, and the use of astrological and cabalistic symbols.[11] Especially did the magico-religious ceremonies of both kinds of magic have overlapping elements. A description of the complex and fastidious procedures of a Renaissance white magician reveals that his ceremony was specifically in conjunction with a particular planet. If, for example, he wished to attract the energies of the sun, all his rites would be timed appropriately for the sun and include: the color of his robes; the material of his altar; the incense burned; and the chants sung.[12]

As for the black magician, he reached a state of "holiness" in his ceremony by fasting, abstaining from sexual intercourse, going without sleep, and meditating upon his task.[13] Special garments, a staff and rod, ablutions, ink and pen, an invocation written in blood, a young goat to be sacrificed, incense, and fumigation were his requirements. A specific day and hour were essential to gain the best planetary response, and a remote, uninhabited location was the most suitable site. Only after offering prayers to God did the black magician conjure up Satan and his demons. Recollecting the wrath of God at their dismissal as rebellious angels from Heaven, the demons hurried to obey. The pact they signed with the magician was written in blood and depended upon exchange and barter, a contest in cunning and guile. With avowedly secular ends in mind, the black magician sought temporal and personal rewards, such as sexual grati-

---

11. Paul H. Kocher, *Science and Religion in Elizabethan England* (San Marino, Calif., 1953), p. 70.
12. Francesco Cattani da Diacetto, *Opera Omnia*, pp. 45–46, quoted in D. P. Walker, *Spiritual Magic from Ficino to Campanella* (London, 1959), p. 33.
13. A. E. Waite, *The Book of Ceremonial Magic* (New Hyde Park, 1961), pp. 13–17 and 24–130.

fication, the location of buried treasure, the control of weather, or the diplomatic secrets and policies of nations. For this pact he was warned never to trespass outside the shelter of his carefully drawn magic circle, even though the demons that he invoked might appear as horrendous apparitions.[14] If he did so, they would end his life im-

> Emperor Lucifer, master of rebellious spirits, I beg you to be favorable to me, when now I call for your minister, the great Lucifuge Rofocale, as I desire to sign a contract with him. . . . O Astaroth, great count, be favorable likewise, and make it possible for the great Lucifuge to appear to me in human form and face, without bad odor, and that he grant me, by the agreement which I am ready to sign with him, all the riches which I need. . . . If you are not willing to come, I will compel you to do so by the power of the great living God, otherwise I will torment you eternally by the power of my mighty words and by the great Key of Solomon, which he used when compelling the rebellious spirits to accept a pact.
>
> (Sanctum Regum, quoted in Kurt Seligmann, *The History of Magic*, New York, 1948, p. 292.)

mediately. Devils were supposed to be heartily resentful of acting in the service of magicians, and only when they had received the promise of a magician's soul would they readily accept bondage to him. Armed with papers that contained his directions for conjuring and his specific demands, the magician stood his ground in the circle, threatening to torture the spirit with the potent words of the Key of Solomon unless he granted the magician the great reward he sought. Whatever the outcome, extreme care and precision were essential, otherwise the magician would be entrapped by the "snares of hell" and lose his soul immediately.

Despite some obvious similarities in their ceremonies, the white magician continued to assert that, unlike the demons of the black magician his daemons were good. So did the Florentine Neoplatonists of the late fifteenth century, who were most responsible for the revival of interest in white magic during the Renaissance. As a reformulated Platonism grafted onto Christianity, Neoplatonism gave rise to a

---

14. One invocation from the *Sanctum Regum* suggests the intractability of black magicians:

system of ideas about the universe through which the white magician sought to refine his soul and gain a direct knowledge of God. Subsequently, his magic not only focused upon contemplation and inner experience but also sought to utilize occult energies within natural objects. At a time when there were attempts at experimentation and codification in natural science, the white magician, who often shared the interests of the natural scientist, also searched for empirical approaches to his art.[15]

In Florence, Ficino speculated on white magic and linked Plato's philosophy to early, ritual mystery cults. What Plato had intended as a dialectic for improving the mind and the soul, Ficino believed was a means through which the individual experienced the presence of God.[16] In his concepts of magic, he also maintained that sound could create stronger astral influences than sight.[17] If there were plants, animals, or stones that more strongly attracted the spiritual influences of a particular planet, there could also be a kind of music that had the same power. Once the magician could create this music by finding the numerical and harmonic proportions suitable to a particular planet, he might expect to evoke a favorable spirit from that source. The magician then would assume the character and power of this planetary spirit.

To a Neoplatonist, this theory of harmony and music was especially acceptable, fitting easily into his framework of a Ptolemaic universe with its music of the spheres, its Pythagorean numerology, and its conception of harmonics as a

15. Ernst Cassirer, *The Individual and the Cosmos in Renaissance Philosophy*, trans. Mario Domandi (New York, 1964), pp. 147–52; Paul O. Kristeller, "Renaissance Platonism," in *Facets of the Renaissance* (New York, 1963), pp. 103–21; *Eight Philosophers of the Italian Renaissance* (Stanford, 1965); Lynn Thorndike, *A History of Magic and Experimental Science,* IV (New York, 1934).
    16. Edgar Wind, *Pagan Mysteries in the Renaissance* (New Haven, 1938), p. 16.
    17. D. P. Walker, *Spiritual Magic from Ficino to Campanella* (London, 1959), p. 1.

link between microcosm and macrocosm.[18] Accompanied by a lyre, Ficino would chant his own version of Orphic hymns,[19] Orpheus being the most potent figure to whom magicians could appeal.[20] To Ficino, Orphic music was intended for Apollo, the Sun God, and was part of a magical rite that also included the use of wine, talismans, and incense. This combination of sight and sound in magic contained parallels with performances in Greek amphitheaters as well as the ceremonies of the Mass. Early Christian borrowings had extended so far as to model the chancel after the early Greek stage.

The Church, of course, inveighed against Ficino's practices. The ritualized performances had obvious parallels to the Roman Catholic Mass: the wearing of robes, the accompaniment of words, music, lights, and the use of wine and incense. The Church, moreover, disapproved of the invocation of daemons.

Despite such ecclesiastical opposition, as Miss Yates has admirably demonstrated, other celebrated Italian philosophers whose interests encompassed white magic still advanced their investigations, often becoming scapegoat figures.[21] More audacious than Ficino, his teacher, Pico declared that white magic was both philosophical and religious, even if pagan in origin. His image of the white magician as a philosopher with divine powers did not save him from the charge of heresy and temporary imprisonment. Bruno, an advanced mystic, returned to the pagan, Egyptian origins of magic, only to be arrested by the Inquisition, imprisoned for ten years, finally accused of heresy, and burned

---

18. See John Hollander, *The Untuning of the Sky: Ideas of Music in English Poetry, 1500–1700* (Princeton, 1961).

19. Pico, *Opera Omnia*, Basiliae, I, 106, quoted in Walker, p. 22. Pico also claimed that in white magic "nothing is more efficacious than the Hymns of Orpheus, if there could be applied to them the suitable music, and disposition of soul, and the other circumstances known to the wise."

20. Cf. Northrop Frye, *A Natural Perspective* (New York, 1965), p. 147.

21. *Giordano Bruno and the Hermetic Tradition.*

at the stake. Unlike Bruno, Della Porta escaped imprisonment through retracting some of his original views in both his *Magica Naturalis,* and later his *Physiognomonia,* when censored by the Inquisition.[22]

In northern Europe, Agrippa endeavored to vindicate magic and had the utopian thought that the best ruler would be a priest-magician heading a theocracy: his attempt to appease the Church was unsuccessful. One who benefited from Agrippa's work was Dr. John Dee, perhaps the best-known practitioner of white magic in England and the unofficial astrologer to Queen Elizabeth. Illustrative of secular opposition, both Burleigh and Walsingham publicly disapproved of Dee's work with spirits. Yet, revealing a curious vein of ambivalence toward magic, Burleigh later wrote to Dee's aide, Kelley, and urged him to place his skills in the service of the queen: "Good Knight, let me end my letter conjuring you, in God's holy name not to keep God's gift from yr natural countrie, but rather to help make Her Majestie a glorious and victorious power against the mallyce of hers and God's enemies."[23] Dying penurious and neglected in 1608, Dee ended a career that had constantly been precarious, misunderstood, and in jeopardy.

The role of the white magician had always been troubled, but by the time of Dee's death the new science of the seventeenth century had opened the way for Mersenne and others to reject magic entirely.[24] And as public interest in white magic waned, churchmen found fewer occasions to voice opposition to it. White magicians as contemplative philosophers had created a unique concept of the universe. The new

---

22. See Louise George Clubb, *Giambattista Della Porta, Dramatist* (Princeton, 1965), pp. 25–26.

23. Quoted in Charlotte Fell-Smith, *John Dee, 1527–1608* (London, 1909), pp. 206–7.

24. In 1625, Marin Mersenne wrote *Quaestiones in Genesim* defending mathematics and science and dismissing the entire magical equipment of plants, statues, stones, along with the use of the cabala and the various hierarchies of angelic power. See Yates, p. 434.

scientists, however, now attempted to assess their own universe, using specific terms that were not mystical.

To what extent the philosophers of white magic were commonplace names in the English Renaissance for audience and playwright may be gauged by the way in which magician-philosophers receive mention in plays. For instance, Johnson knew of Dee. In *The Alchemist* Subtle conjures with the white magician's name while he is advising Abel Drugger of a favorable sign for his store:

> He first shall haue a bell, that's ABEL;
> And by it, standing one, whose name is DEE,
> In a rugg gowne; there's D, and *Rug,* that's DRVG:
> And right anenst him, a Dog snarling *Er;*
> There's DRVGGER, ABEL DRVGGER. That's his signe.
> And here's now mysterie and hieroglyphick!
> (II, iv, 19–24)[25]

Marlowe mentions Agrippa as if he were a household word, for Faustus claims that he:

> Will be as cunning as Agrippa was,
> Whose shadows made all Europe honor him.
> (i, 116–17)

Even though he does not name him, Shakespeare possibly recollected the career of Dee as he gathered a background for Prospero.

In general, however, white magic in the Renaissance remained a covert activity, repressed by the Church. Not surprisingly did its findings remain the property of initiates: philosophers whose manuscripts were published took pains to conceal significant discoveries. In England, a few of the cognoscenti had heard of the Florentine Neoplatonists through translations and word of mouth. Free of the In-

---

25. I use the Herford and Simpson edition for all quotations from Ben Jonson's works (Jonson, 5:338).

quisition, white magic could survive there in a somewhat more tolerant atmosphere, though this hardly put the subject in the public domain. More familiar were those legendary prototype figures whose lives embraced wonder-working and white magic.

2
The Legendary Magician

*I*n considering the mysterious and controversial figure
of the magician for use on the stage, the playwright of
the English Renaissance drew heavily on inherited views of
magic, views that were constantly being introduced into
the oral tradition of folklore. Such real and legendary proto-
typic figures as Faustus, Moses, and Solomon were fundamental to this tradition. Contemporary public sources, of
course, did contribute to a common storehouse of knowledge.
First of all, there was the powerful organ of the pulpit,
from which spread the fearful admonition "Thou shalt not
suffer a witch to live."[1] Second, earlier drama inevitably
brought with it fictional and popular concepts of magic. As
a third source, the pamphlets and penny sheets of the day
held an immeasurable treasury of folklore tradition.[2] And
last, popular prose narrative, whether novella, satire, or
short story, contained still further aspects of folklore be-

---

1. See Gerald Owst, *Literature and Pulpit in Medieval England* (Cambridge, 1933).
2. Autolycus includes such sheets in his sales. See *The Winter's Tale*
(IV, iii and iv).

lief. Yet, archetypal to all these sources were the legendary figures, whose stories contained such devices as the magic circle, the ring, the renunciation of magic, or the magicians' contest, any of which the playwright might happily use in the construction of his plot.

Inside the magic circle, for example, Faustus invokes Mephistophilis through the use of cabalistic signs and astrology:

> Within this circle is Jehovah's name,
> Forward and backward anagrammatized,
> The breviated names of holy saints,
> Figures of every adjunct to the heavens,
> And characters and signs of erring stars
> By which the spirits are enforced to rise.
>   (I, iii, 8–13)[3]

Nor does the "charmed circle" exist only for the black magician. In *The Tempest,* when Ariel leads the spellbound King's party to Prospero, stage directions state that they "stand charm'd" within the circle that Prospero has drawn until they are released through the restorative powers of heavenly music. Jacques's satirical baiting of his fellow exiles in the forest of Arden in *As You Like It* is another instance of the magic circle:

> If it do come to pass
> That any man turn ass,
> Leaving his wealth and ease,
> A stubborn will to please,
> Ducdame, ducdame, ducdame:
> Here shall he see
> Gross fools as he
> An if he will come to me.
>   (II, v, 52–59)

He calls "fools into a circle" by using the Greek word

---

3. Christopher Marlowe, *Doctor Faustus,* in *Elizabethan and Stuart Plays,* ed. Charles Baskerville et al. (New York, 1934).

ducdame (I foretell), which carries implications of astrology and fortunetelling. To an Elizabethan audience, the most familiar magician was Doctor Faustus. Marlowe probed his legend, exploiting the overall potentialities of the theatrical interpretation of magic to a degree that no playwright bettered. Faustus captured the public imagination to such an extent that at one performance, when he uttered an actual spell in Latin onstage, William Prynne made record of

> the visible apparition of the Devill on the stage at the Belsauvage Playhouse in Queene Elizabeths day, (to the great amazement of both the Actors and Spectators) whiles they were profanely playing the History of Faustus (the truth of which I have heard from many now alive, who well remember it) there being some distracted with that fearful sight.[4]

In the minds of most of the audience, Faustus was a witch, for, as Dalton suggests:

> The witch dealeth rather by a friendly and voluntary Conference or Agreement between him (or her) and the Devil or Familiar, to have his turn served; and in lieu thereof the Witch giveth (or offereth) his or her Soul, Blood, or other gift unto the Devil.[5]

Through a pact whose eventual fruits are graphically clear, Faustus seeks power, wealth, prestige, and a knowledge of the unknown, a choice at opposite poles from that of the selfless white magician. And does not Faustus disappear into the mouth of Hell, where recalcitrant sinners were sent in medieval miracle plays?

Like Circe, Medea, or subsequent enchantresses in literature who act to control nature, he orders Mephistophilis

> To do whatever Faustus shall command,
> Be it to make the moon drop from her sphere
> Or the ocean to overwhelm the world.
> (iii, 40–42)

---

4. William Prynne, *Histriomastix* (1633), p. 556.
5. Michael Dalton, *The Countrey Justice* (1677), pp. 385-86.

His intentions are further clarified as he fearlessly chooses evil demons to support his work:

> There is no chief but only Beelzebub,
> To whom Faustus doth dedicate himself.
> The word "damnation" terrifies him not . . .
>
> (iii, 60–62)

Making heretical, grandiose claims to be "emperor of the world," he bases his power on a compact with Lucifer that allows him the control of nature for twenty-four years, and then, having "incurr'd eternal death," he must surrender his soul. Mephistophilis rejoices at claiming Faustus's soul for Hell, and the morality figure of the Good Angel reminds the unrepentant sinner that salvation is impossible without faith and grace.

Many in the audience must have reacted with ambivalent feelings to the conflict between the attractive superhuman aims of the black magician and their own moral background. Others must have judged that the arrogance, willfulness, and atheism of the unrepentant Faustus merited punishment, agreeing with the Chorus's terse comment:

> Faustus is gone: regard his hellish fall
> Whose fiendful fortune may exhort the wise
> Only to wonder at unlawful things,
> Whose deepness doth entice such forward wits
> To practise more than heavenly power permits.
>
> (xv, 146–50)

The opposite of his black counterpart, the white magician forever sought the eventual goal of his soul's salvation. Dedicated to beneficent acts that would bring about the well-being of others, his legendary and mythological prototypes provided the playwright with suitable themes for the public stage and the court masque. Such magicians were often prophet (Zoroaster), priest (Moses), or king (Solomon), and wielded power comparable to that of mythological gods.

For the most part benevolent, their magic dramatically re-ordered the course of nature, fulfilling functions similar to those of the witch doctor or medicine man, who assured his tribe of rain, crops, fertility, victory, freedom from disease, and an auspicious future.[6]

Zoroaster, one of the earliest known of such magician figures, was regarded as the Prophet of Iran and believed to have supernatural powers for curing diseases, fending off ferocious animals, bringing rain, and preventing crop blight through magical rites. Moses, however, demonstrated his skills to prove that the all-powerful God was on his side, and also to destroy the enemies of the Israelites. By miracu-lously producing water and food in the desert, he also revealed himself as the tribal medicine man.[7]

The Bible was a major source of ancient figures with magical powers, such as Solomon, to whom God granted an understanding heart so as to better judge his people. Apocry-phal stories accumulated around such figures. Some imputed to Solomon the use of black magic: captive demons built in his temple a magical throne, beneath which they were supposed to have concealed books that they might later accuse him of using black magic. On another occasion, and despite his prodigious wisdom, Solomon allowed the demon Asmodeus to usurp his power by taking his magic ring that he had tossed into the sea. Only after repentance did he retrieve his power, regain his ring, and dispose of the demon.[8]

The magic ring was a common possession of the legendary magician, and as a source of power or a talisman could bring fertility and health, act as a preventive, or fend off death. Solomon's particular ring was made of four stones

---

6. E. M. Butler, *The Myth of the Magus* (Cambridge, 1948), p. 2. See also Raphael Patai and Robert Graves, *Hebrew Myths: the book of Genesis* (Garden City, N.Y., 1964).

7. Butler, *Magus*, pp. 29–34.

8. *Ibid.*, pp. 35–43.

and was believed to provide him with control over nature, animals, and all types of spirits.[9]

Such rings often became key plot devices for Elizabethan playwrights. Though not described in detail, the magic ring in *The Wisdome of Dr. Dodypoll* (1599), possessed by Lucilia's father, enables him to overcome the black magic of the Enchanter. In *A Pleasant Comedy called the Two Merry Milkmaids* (1619), the turning point of the play focuses upon a ring that makes the wearer invisible. A spirit gives it to Landoffe, the magician, who instructs the courtier, Dorilus, in its use. With this aid, Dorilus pleads in court for an unjustly accused defendant, his disembodied voice creating such awe that he wins the case.

The Elizabethan playwrights also drew upon another important act of Solomon, the burning of all his books on magic shortly before he died. Magicians in literature appear to have a tradition of destroying their books, following the same course taken by actual magicians in times of crisis or when their magic was renounced. Simon Magus, for example, drowned his books so that St. Peter could not accuse him of sorcery.[10] Roger Bacon burned his books. John Dee also made the same claim, though it is likely that his medium, Edward Kelley, who was in charge of their burning, kept them and later arranged a spurious "miracle" of their restoration.

As far as the dramatists were concerned, such renunciations merely made the magician a more exciting figure for the stage. That Faustus refuses to consent to such a renunciation before his time has run out provides a suspense-filled climax to *Doctor Faustus,* setting the stage for the Old Man and Mephistophilis to battle over the magician's soul. The Old Man urges Faustus to repent and receive salvation:

---

9. See J. R. McCarthy, *Rings Through the Ages* (New York, 1945), pp. 45–46.
10. E. M. Butler, *Ritual Magic* (Cambridge, 1949), p. 268.

Break heart, drop blood, and mingle it with tears,
Tears falling from repentant heaviness
Of thy most vile and loathsome filthiness,
The stench whereof corrupts the inward soul
With such flagitious crimes of heinous sins
As no commiseration may expel,
But mercy, Faustus, of thy Savior sweet,
Whose blood alone must wash away thy guilt.
(XIV, 42–49)

Faustus pays no heed, remaining with Mephistophilis, at which the Old Man chides the magician:

Accursed Faustus, miserable man,
That from thy soul exclud'st the grace of heaven,
And fliest the throne of his tribunal seat.
(XIV, 113–15)

An eventual offer to burn his books to gain a last-minute reprieve is too late; Faustus is consigned to Hell.

Friar Bacon's renunciation is no less spectacular. Having used demons, apparently without making a compact with the Devil, Bacon forsakes his powers when his magic causes the death of two students he had wished to help. He then repents and seeks salvation.[11]

Bacon, thy magic doth effect this massacre.
This glass perspective worketh many woes.
And therefore, seeing these brave, lusty brutes,
These friendly youths did perish by thine art,
End all thy magic and thine art at once.
. . . .
I tell thee, Bungay, it repents me sore
That ever Bacon meddled in his art.
The hours I have spent in pyromantic spells,
The fearful tossing in the latest night
Of papers full of nigromantic charms.
Conjuring and abjuring devils and fiends
With stole and albe and strange pentaganon,

11. Robert Greene, *Friar Bacon and Friary Bungay*, ed. Daniel Seltzer (Lincoln, Neb., 1963).

> The wresting of the holy name of God,
> As Sother, Eloim, and Andonai,
> Alpha, Manoth, and Tetragrammaton,
> With praying to the five-fold powers of heaven,
> Are instances that Bacon must be damn'd
> For using devils to countervail his God.
>
> (XIII, 75–79, 85–97)

Here Bacon shows that he has conducted his ceremonies in priestly garb, alb and stole, and focused on the cabala and the sephiroth to master the multiple meanings of the words for God.[12] But he avoids falling into despair, the problem of Faustus, "Sins have their salves. Repentance can do much," and he abruptly abandons his black magic, undoubtedly to the satisfaction of much of the audience:

> . . . I'll spend the remnant of my life
> In pure devotion, praying to my God
> That he would save what Bacon vainly lost.
>
> (XV, 106–8)

Elsewhere, in *The Rare Triumphs of Love and Fortune* (1582, attributed to Anthony Munday), Hermione encounters his long-lost father, Bomelio, a wrongly exiled courtier, who as a hermit now studies magic. Alone in his father's cave, Hermione uncovers books about magic, discourses on the danger of their blasphemous contents, and burns them, asking the audience to abhor the magician's art as much as he does. Hoping to use magic to further his son's happiness with the King's daughter, Bomelio goes mad when he discovers the loss of his books. On regaining his sanity, and presumably having renounced his magic, he is once more accepted at court.

Another exiled courtier, Prospero in *The Tempest,* possesses a magic that is more concerned with daemons than that of the previous three magicians. He retains it, however,

---

12. "Sother . . . Tetragrammaton." These letter combinations spelled the divine names of God and were supposed to contain miraculous powers. The Pentagon had the name of God at each of its five points.

only so long as he requires it to cure his enemies of their disorders and forgive them:

> But this rough magic
> I here abjure; and when I have requir'd
> Some heavenly music (which even now I do)
> To work mine end upon their senses, that
> This airy charm is for, I'll break my staff,
> Bury it certain fathoms in the earth,
> And deeper than did ever plummet sound
> I'll drown my book.
>
> (V, i, 50–57)

Returning to the urbane society of his court, he then faces old age and death.

Through his wonder-working and healing, the figure of Christ appears as the legendary white magician par excellence. In the New Testament Christ resists Satan's temptation to perform black magical tricks as a show of power. His miracles, however, may be associated with benevolent feats considered magical in different contexts by men of later ages. Quite possibly, white magicians saw their own healing powers, though hardly equivalent, as having a goal similar to Christ's. The New Testament shows Christ curing the blind and the dumb and casting out devils. He miraculously creates an abundance of food from very little, transforms water into wine, and produces a gigantic haul of fish, all actions reminiscent of the tribal magician figure who ensured his people of a continued supply of food. Incidentally, the Apocrypha contains episodes in the childhood of Christ that also involved His use of magic.

According to legend, a magician named Simon Magus stood in heretical opposition to Christ, setting himself up as the transcendent god of a gnostic cosmos.[13] After studying

---

13. Butler, *Magus*, pp. 73–78. See *A Dictionary of the Bible*, ed. James Hastings (New York, 1902), 6:520–27, for the different sources of the legends of Simon Magus. See also Rudolph Bultmann, *Primitive Christianity in its Contemporary Setting* (New York, 1956), pp. 162–71; Hans Jonas, *The Gnostic Religion* (Boston, 1958), and Robert M. Grant, *Gnosticism: a source book of heretical writings from the early Christian period* (New York, 1961).

magic in Egypt, he became the leader of a sect and claimed that only through his own intervention as a figure of redemption might souls be elevated from the lower world into which they had fallen from heaven. An important event for later literature was his famous contest with St. Peter, arranged by the Emperor Nero when Peter asserted that he was one of Christ's disciples and Simon a mere magician. To prove his point during a contest over who could fly to heaven, Peter challenged the demons that aided Simon in his flight, and Simon immediately fell to the ground.

Creating, as they did, theatrical suspense as well as an aura of spectacle and wonder, these dramatic contests between magicians became a recurring feature in both the Elizabethan theater and Jacobean court masques. Although the events are not actually dramatized in *The Tempest,* Prospero's initial struggle with the witch Sycorax for control of the enchanted isle was just such a contest—with Prospero's white magic defeating the black magic of the witch. In the Jacobean court masque, black magic often appeared as the predominant agent—the enchanter typifying chaotic forces, the Circe-Medea figure, a pagan enchantress acting strictly from evil motives. In triumphant opposition, kings and mythological gods acted as agents far more potent than white magicians, and rescued the spellbound masquers.

Several of the magician contests depend upon an interplay of black and white magic, polarities that obviously create a potential dramatic conflict, even though distinctions between the two might remain blurred. Many such details, in fact, were so recondite that they were beyond the grasp or interest of ordinary playgoers, and judging from the plays, beyond those of the ordinary playwright too. Nonetheless, the basic principles of magical practice, black and white, clearly were well understood by much of the general populace.

Other significant contests occur in *Friar Bacon and Friar*

Bungay (1589), *John A Kent and John A Cumber* (1589), *Henry IV,* Part I (1597), and *The Birth of Merlin* (1608). In Robert Greene's *Friar Bacon and Friar Bungay,* Bacon's magic impedes the speech of his fellow magician, Bungay, so that in his role of friar he cannot complete a marriage ceremony he is performing. Instead, he is carried off on the back of a devil. Later, before a royal audience, Bungay accepts the challenge of Vandermast, a German magician. The contest begins with Vandermast's defense of the spirits of pyromancy (divination by fire), and Bungay's defense of the spirits of geomancy (divination from the pattern a handful of earth makes when it is thrown on the ground).[14] In the ensuing rhetorical debate, Vandermast reasons with the aid of the cabalists, "Hermes, Melchie, and Pythagoras," who claim that earth is the least important of the four elements. He also cites Hermes as an authority in offering his proof that the spirits of fire are greater than those of earth. Bungay rejects this argument and also calls on Hermes, claiming that

> 　　　　　　　magic haunts the grounds,
> And those strange necromantic spells,
> That work such shows and wondering in the world,
> Are acted by those geomantic spirits
> That Hermes calleth *terrae filii.*
> 　　　　　　　　　　　　(ix, 46–50)

Moreover, he argues that spirits in the earth are bound to be stronger than "fiery spirits that are but transparent shades." Vandermast counters that earthly spirits are most likely to be Lucifer's, having been thrown to the "center of the earth," only to serve "jugglers, witches, and vile sorcerers."

Bungay then conjures up the golden tree from the garden of the Hesperides, which emerges through the stage trap door. Not to be outdone, Vandermast materializes Hercu-

---

14. Greene, *Friar Bacon and Friar Bungay,* pp. 52–60.

les, who breaks the branches of the tree. Bungay cannot match this and the German magician now boasts that

> Bungay is learned enough to be a friar,
> But to compare with Jacques Vandermast,
> Oxford and Cambridge must go seek their cells
> To find a man to match him in his art.
>
> (ix, 106–9)

At this point, Bacon replaces the defeated Bungay and renders Hercules powerless to carry out further orders:

> Bacon, that bridles headstrong Belcephon,
> And rules Asmenoth, guider of the north,
> Binds me from yielding unto Vandermast.
>
> (ix, 141–43)

Vandermast is amazed:

> Never before was't known to Vandermast
> That men held devils in such obedient awe.
> Bacon doth more than art, or else I fail.
>
> (ix, 145–47)

As final proof of his superiority, Bacon orders the spirit of Hercules to "transport the German into Hapsburg straight, that he may learn by travail . . . more secret dooms and aphorisms of art."

Bacon's powers are to be admired as an entertainment, and even though he conjures with the demons, Belcephon and Asmenoth, there is no mention of damnation up to this point in the play. Later, however, he renounces his liaison with demons and in repentance vows to devote himself to God.

The motivating force behind *John A Kent and John A Cumber*,[15] written by Anthony Munday, is the magician contest. Here, John a Kent, a Welsh sorcerer, employs

---

15. Anthony Munday, *John A Kent and John A Cumber*, ed. Muriel St. Clare Byrne, The Malone Society Reprints (Oxford, 1923).

magic to unite two pairs of lovers whose willful fathers disallow their union, having other matches in mind for them. The fathers, in turn, hire the Scottish magician, John a Cumber, who enthusiastically pits his skill against his Welsh counterpart, both using the loving couples as pawns in their game of magical ploys. John a Kent is aided by his spirit-fairy, Shrimp, who is almost a prototype for Ariel. Versatile, swift, and clever, Shrimp, like Ariel, can make himself invisible and play such enchanted music on his pipes that he can lure the listener to follow him through the woods, or lull him to sleep. With this music, in fact, he successfully conducts the lovers to a rendezvous far from the effects of John a Cumber's spells.

In the end, the slur of black magic is cast upon John a Cumber, "that overreachte the deuill by his skill." John a Kent, by "his wit and art," however, promises the true lovers that he will effect their union without any danger. The magicians conduct their contest by disguising as one another and then leading their mutual clients astray, until John a Cumber eventually admits defeat. A final trick of John a Kent unites all four lovers for their marriages inside Chester Abbey. In this way, the white magician reaffirms the natural order of true love in society and denounces the contrived unnatural plans of the parents.

Another Welsh magician, Owen Glendower, appears in Shakespeare's *Henry IV*, Part I. He creates tempests to prevent the invasion of Wales, and provoked by Hotspur, who doubts his powers and taunts him as a charlatan, conducts a pseudo-contest. Hotspur's skepticism is silenced when Glendower, in a Welsh invocation, calls for music from players who "hang in the air a thousand leagues from hence," and then "music is heard."

Two separate contests exist in *The Birth of Merlin*,[16] which was written by William Rowley, possibly in conjunction with Shakespeare. Initially, Anselme, a saintly British

---

16. Students' Facsimile Edition (n.p., n.d.).

hermit, overwhelms the Saxon magician, Proximus. When Proximus conjures up Hector and Achilles for a spectacle of their fighting prowess, Anselme stops them in their tracks and they flee. Asserting that his Christian powers are far more potent than the conjurer's pagan magic, Anselme claims victory.

Later, Proximus challenges the young Merlin, whose reputation is at stake because he is the child of the Devil and the peasant Joan Goe-too't. His life, moreover, is sought by the usurping King, who is building a castle in Wales. Each day, however, the castle's foundations crumble and prophecies of other wizards claim that "it can never stand, till the foundations laid with Mortar be temper'd with the fatal blood of such a childe, whose father was no mortal." When Merlin is summoned, he realizes that he may be the victim. Through his superior magic, he escapes death, conjuring a stone that falls on Proximus and kills him. With the aid of a wand, he reveals to the King the reason why his castle is unstable: two dragons have been fighting in a cave beneath its foundations. Merlin's diagnosis and prognostication point to the tyrant King, who will be defeated by Prince Uther Pendragon for having usurped the throne of Uther's brother. At this outcome, Uther gratefully declares "thine art hath made such proof, that we believe thy words authentical, be ever neer us, my Prophet, and the Guide of all my actions." Merlin dutifully responds, "My service shall be faithful to your person, and all my studies for my countries safety," and remains by Uther as he restores the kingdom.

Merlin's legend was the original creation of Geoffrey of Monmouth in *Historia Regum Britanniae* (1135-1147) and *Vita Merlini* (1148), and the play largely follows Geoffrey's story. Though a magician of fiction, Merlin held an important place in popular medieval thought; indeed, the need for a court magician was still relevant at the time of Elizabeth, whose adviser, as mentioned earlier, was the astrologist, Dr. Dee. The general public also expressed its strong desire for a tribal medicine man by endowing a figure like Merlin with lifelike attributes far beyond his fictional sources. And in the eleventh century, a thousand years after Virgil's death, a belief that he had possessed superhuman powers was bestowed upon the poet. His prophecy of the coming of Christ in the fourth of the *Eclogues* was evidence, though some sought further proof of his unique powers in his description of Dido's magical funeral ceremony in the *Aeneid*. Not surprising, therefore, is the accumulation in Renaissance culture of stories about legendary magicians, among them those containing the inherited views of magic and wonder-working that were eminently suitable for playwrights.

3

Healers in Shakespeare

*T*aking as an endorsement the biblical admonition that

> The Lord hath created medicines out of the earth; and he that is wise will not abhor them,
>
> (Eccles. 38:4)

the white magician of Shakespeare's time sometimes assumed the role of healer, deriving his medicines from the extracted properties of plants, animals, and minerals. Through the technical processes he used in trying to discover the sympathetic energies of tangible things, a fundamental aspect of white magic, the healer contributed substantially to the advancement of natural science. Nonetheless, the healer's role, like other roles the white magician might assume, was still regarded with ambivalence. This was so partly because the technical processes he employed were also commonly used in alchemy, and partly because, prior to the general use of scientific terminology for identifying properties in tangible objects, healing had the aura of wonder-working. Today's distinctions did not exist and consequently magic and medicine so overlapped that cures often appeared to be the result of occult wisdom. It is not surprising then, that Shakespeare, in his healer figures, declines to draw a line between magic and medicine.

The art of healing in Shakespeare is in most cases bound up with the remedies of folk medicine that were documented in herbals.[1] As late as the mid-seventeenth century, Nicholas Culpeper, in *The Complete Herbal,* drew upon theories of white magic in stating his views of cures:

> I knew well enough the whole world, and everything in it, was formed of a composition of contrary elements, and in such harmony as must needs show the wisdom and power of a great god. I knew as well this creation, though thus composed of contraries, was one united body, and man an epitome of it: I knew those various affections in man, in respect of sickness and health, were caused naturally (though God may have other ends best known to himself) by the various operations of the Microcosm: and I would not be ignorant, that as the cause is, so must the cure be; and therefore he that would know the operation of the Herbs, must look up high as the Stars, astrologically; I have always found the disease vary according to the various motions of the stars; and this is enough, one would think, to teach a man by the effect where the cause lies. Then to find out the reason of the operation of Herbes, Plants, etc., by the Stars went I.[2]

---

1. As early as the first century A.D., Dioscorides had produced a herbal anatomizing the properties of six hundred plants. His influence was to be found throughout the following centuries, culminating in Elizabethan herbals. These included Richard Bankes's *Herball* (1525), *The Grete Herball* (1526), printed by Peter Treveris, *Macer's Herball* (*c.* 1530), *A Newe Herball* (1551), by William Turner, *The Garden of Health, Conteyning Vertues and Properties of Simples and Plants* (1579), and *Gerard's Herball* (1597). The advancement of humanism brought a fresh examination of Dioscorides and pharmacological concepts. For example, a plant such as Verbena was thought to cure both the plague and epilepsy. It was included in *The Grete Herball* so as to inform the reader of its "gracyous vertues" and which parts of the body it would best affect: Verbena. It is otherwise called columbina. It is colde and drye. . . . To all swellynges of the necke . . . the root of this herbe hanged about his necke profyteth moche. . . . For the payne of those that is in the brest, take the powdre of this herbe that was gadred when the sonne was at the hyest and if the pacyent can go give hime v spones full . . . with warm wyne (London: printed by Peter Treveris, 1526), p. 49.
2. Epistle to the Reader (London, 1653).

Culpeper stipulated, moreover, that the healer should diagnose disease through astrology and select special days for his cures accordingly, both of which actions were reminiscent of white magic:

> First, consider what planet causeth the diseases; that thou mayest find it in my aforesaid judgment of Diseases. Secondly, consider what part of the body is afflicted by the disease, and whether in the flesh, or blood, or ventricles.
> Thirdly, consider by what planet the afflicted part of the body is governed: that my judgment of Diseases will inform you also. Fourthly, You may oppose diseases by Herbes of the planet, opposite to the planet that causes them: as diseases by Jupiter by Herbes of Mercury, and the disease of the Luminaries by the Herbs of Saturn, and the contrary; diseases of Mars by Herbs of Venus, and the contrary. Fifthly, There is a way to cure diseases sometimes by Sympathy and so every planet cures his own disease; as the Sun and Moon by their Herbs cure the Eyes, Saturn the Spleen, Jupiter the Liver, Mars the Gall and diseases of choler, and Venus diseases in the Instruments of Generation.[3]

Hippocrates, Galen, and Avicenna all endorsed the use of herbs for curing disease, advising healers to understand the Pythagorean theory of critical days in illness and also the "doctrine of humors," because disease altered the regular proportions of the body's four fluids. By holding to dogmatic views on the four humors and a preference for philosophic rather than empiric proofs, Galen retarded a more objective kind of investigation and perpetuated many basic medical misconceptions. In the sixteenth century, however, Galen's theories were challenged by Paracelsus, who, concerned more with experience and objectivity than with dogma, stated that the elements of a man's body were composed of salt, mercury, and sulphur. Specific properties of plants, he claimed, were to be gauged by the proportions of their particular elements. "The art of prescribing medicines consists in extracting and not in compounding, . . .

---

3. *Ibid.*

in the discovery of that which is concealed, and not in compounding various things and piecing them together."[4] The
goal of both alchemist and physician was, of course, to raise
a property to perfection, and their tasks thus bore distinct
similarities. This was especially so in searching for the most
renowned of all arcana, the philosopher's stone, which was
reputed to have powers of purifying and rejuvenating the
whole human body.

Nonetheless, Paracelsus applied the concept of humors
to the actual classification of plants and categorized them
as hot or cold, dry or moist, to the first, second, third, or
fourth degree.[5] With Galen, he believed that the power of
a plant depended upon its appearance and that its fruit,
leaves, or roots might resemble a part of the body or some
phase of the disease about to be treated.[6] According to this
"doctrine of signatures," outward form provided clues to
internal properties. Della Porta, as well as other philosophers of white magic, also subscribed to the "doctrine,"
accounting, no doubt, for the many illustrations in herbals
of the emblematic details that were essential to it.[7]

More important to the healer than a study of the appearance of plants was a familiarity with astrology, for astrolo-
gers, according to Culpeper, "are the only men I know that
are fit to study physic, physic without astrology being like
a lamp without oil."[8] He advised the healer to fortify and
cure the body with sympathetic medicines "of the nature of
the sign ascending." Above all, the healer should "regard
the heat, keep that upon the wheels, because the Sun is the
foundation of life, and therefore those universal remedies,

---

4. Paracelsus, *Selected Writings,* ed. Jolande Jacobi, trans. Norbert
Guterman (New York, 1951), p. 164.
5. C. F. Leyel, *The Magic of Herbs* (London, 1932), p. 73.
6. Arturo Castiglioni, *Adventures of the Mind* (New York, 1946), pp.
76-77.
7. See Giambattista Della Porta, *Physiognomonica* (Naples, 1538).
8. Culpeper, pp. 210-11.

Aurum Potabile, and the Philosopher's Stone, cure all disorders by fortifying the heart."[9]

The closeness of the physician's, herbalist's, and healer's arts makes it possible for many analogies to be drawn between them and the craft of the white magician and wonderworker. Shakespeare utilizes this overlapping to create several characters who function as both healers and wonderworkers; their role is not that of white magician (Prospero is Shakespeare's unique example), but their actions suggest an awareness of white magic.

Plant cures, for example, are used or referred to several times in Shakespeare: the Doctor in *King Lear* assures Cordelia that there "are many simples operative whose power will close the eye of anguish," and her reply invokes from him,

> All blest secrets
> All you unpublish'd virtues of the earth,
> Spring with my tears! be aidant and remediate
> In the good man's distress!
>
> (IV, iv, 13–14)

Cleopatra calls for mandragora, the juice of the mandrake, which was supposed to be found growing beneath the gallows, "that I might sleep out this great gap of time my Antony is away" (I, v. 5). When in *Love's Labour's Lost,* Costard breaks his shin, he asks for a plantain, whose juicy, bruised leaves contain healing and cooling properties (II, i, 74-75). Plantain, otherwise called "waybroad," was listed in an early recipe book as being capable of curing twenty-two diseases: "If a man ache in half his head . . . delve upon Waybroad without iron ere the rising of the sun, bind the roots about the head with Crosswort by a red fillet, soon he will be well."[10]

Privately experiencing the first pangs of love for Bene-

---

9. *Ibid.*
10. Quoted in H. N. Ellacombe, *The Plant-lore and Garden-craft of Shakespeare* (London, 1878), p. 216.

dick, Beatrice in *Much Ado About Nothing* is unable to
express them and complains of being "stuffed and unable
to smell." With a playful pun, Margaret advises her to
"get you some of this distilled Carduus Benedictus, and lay
it to your heart: it is the only thing for a qualm" (III, iv,
73-75). Carduus is a genus of prickly herbs that were
supposed to cure head pains and "comforteth vitall spirits."[11]

A Shakespearean character who displays a knowledge of
herbs approaching a white magician's expertise is Friar
Laurence in *Romeo and Juliet*. Monasteries often planted
herb gardens during the Middle Ages so that monks could
concoct curative medicines.[12] In the second act Friar Laurence is discovered at dawn in his cell, about to visit one:

> Now, ere the sun advance his burning eye,
> The day to cheer and night's dark dew to dry,
> I must up-fill this osier cage of ours
> With baleful weeds and precious-juiced flowers,
> The earth that's nature's mother is her tomb;
> What is her burying grave that is her womb,
> And from her womb children of divers kind
> We sucking on her natural bosom find,
> Many for many virtues excellent,
> None but for some and yet all different.
> O, mickle is the powerful grace that lies
> In herbs, plants, stones, and their true qualities:
> For nought so vile that on the earth doth live
> But to the earth some special good doth give,
> Nor ought so good but strain's from that fair use
> Revolts from true birth, stumbling on abuse.
> (II, iii, 5–20)

Although no astrological concept is developed, Friar
Laurence carefully selects the most auspicious time of day

11. William Langham, *The Garden of Health* (London, 1579).
12. Leyel, p. 41. Shakespeare displays an extensive knowledge of plants
(See H. N. Ellacombe, p. 381). For *The Tempest* alone, Ellacombe finds
the following plants mentioned: apple, crab, wheat, rye, barley, vetches,
oats, peas, briar, furze, gorse, thorns, broom, cedar, corn, cowslip, nettle,
docks, mallow, filbert, heath, ling, grass, nut, ivy, lily, piony, lime, mush-
rooms, oak, acorn, pignuts, pine, reed, saffrom, sedges, vines.

for collecting herbs and flowers. All things on earth, he declares, whether herbs, plants, or stones, possess unique and useful properties available to those who seek them. The wonder-worker's kinship with nature becomes more apparent as Friar Laurence discourses on the dual nature of the flower he holds, one part poisonous and the other medicinal. He is using this dichotomy to debate the duality of grace and will within man when Romeo bursts in upon him, an act that to the old man can mean only one thing— a change in the state of the four humors within Romeo.

Later, the Friar prescribes to the distraught Juliet a narcotic that will create the semblance of death:

> Take thou this vial, being then in bed,
> And this distilled liquor drink thou off;
> When presently through all thy veins shall run
> A cold and drowsy humour, for no pulse
> Shall keep his native progress, but surcease:
> No warmth, no breath, shall testify thou livest;
> The roses in thy lips and cheeks shall fade
> To paly ashes, thy eyes' windows fall,
> Like death when he shuts up the day of life;
> Each part, deprived of supple government
> Shall, stiff and stark and cold, appear like death.
> (IV, i, 93–103)[13]

Since the narcotic is intended for a beneficent outcome, it might be seen as a use of white magic by some of the audience.

---

13. Although mandragora was a familiar pain-killer and dormative in the Middle Ages, the Physicians of Myddrai had also discovered their own sleeping potion to encourage sleep during operations:
Drink the juice of orpine, eringo, poppy, mandrake, ground ivy, hemlock, and lettuce, of each equal parts. Let clean earth be mixed with them, and a potion prepared, then without doubt the patient will sleep. . . . When you wish to awake him, let a sponge be pounded in vinegar and put in his nostrils. If you wish that he should not awake for four days, get a penny weight of the wax from a dog's ear and the same quantity of pitch. Administer it to the patient and he will sleep (quoted in Leyel, p. 144; the Physicians of Myddrai's recipe for sleeping potion).

The audience may also have responded to the suggestive parallel between Friar Laurence and the Mantuan apothecary who sells the poison to Romeo at the beginning of the fifth act. Apothecaries were usually thought to aid in curing sickness and they certainly extracted properties from plants, minerals, and animals to make up their drugs. Shakespeare, however, is careful to particularize this apothecary by emphasizing his extreme poverty:

> Famine is in thy cheeks,
> Need and oppression starveth in thine eyes,
> Contempt and beggary hangs upon thy back.
> (V, i, 69–71)

Because of this poverty he sells the poison illegally, diverging from the more familiar benevolent image of the apothecary.

Just as Juliet is discovered in apparent death, so in *Cymbeline*, Imogen, the recipient of a similar narcotic, also appears to be dead. In this play, Cornelius, a court physician to Imogen's stepmother, the Queen, has provided the Queen with his considerable knowledge of herbal practices. She orders her ladies "whiles yet the dew's on ground, gather those flowers; make haste: who has the note of them?" (I, v, 1-2), and then she asks Cornelius whether he has brought with him certain drugs, which he describes as being "most poisonous compounds, which are movers of a languishing death." The Queen defends her need, claiming that as a "longtime pupil" of Cornelius, she wishes to experiment with the drugs upon animals, though not upon humans. When Cornelius warns her that "these effects will be both noisome and infectious," she cursorily dismisses him. In an aside, Cornelius reveals a deep awareness of the Queen's character:

> I do know her spirit,
> And will not trust one of her malice with

A drug of such damn'd nature. Those she
Will stupify and dull the sense awhile;
Then afterward up higher: but there is
No danger in what show of death it makes,
More than the locking-up the spirits, a time,
To be more fresh reviving. She is fool'd
With a most false effect; and I the truer,
So to be false with her.

(I, v, 34–44)

To protect her from her stepmother, who plans to poison
her, Cornelius gives Imogen a drug that makes her appear
dead; but she reawakens when the potion wears off. In the
final scene, Cornelius reveals how he had substituted a
harmless narcotic for the poison in order to foil the Queen's
plot. He tells Cymbeline, moreover, that she confessed to
having a poison for him as well:

I dreading that her purpose
Was of more danger, did compound for her
A certain stuff, which, being ta'en, would cease
The present power of life, but in short time
All offices of nature should again
Do their due functions.

(V, v, 253–58)

Cornelius emerges from the play as a worker for benevolent ends who refuses to entrust the full knowledge of his
herbal practice to the Queen, knowing that she would only
have used it for evil.

Another healer who uses his skills to bring about fruitful
ends is Cerimon in *Pericles*. While at sea, Thaisa, the wife
of Pericles, apparently dies following the birth of their
child Marina, and, at the sailors' insistence is placed in a
coffin and thrown overboard. Hours later, the coffin is
washed up in Ephesus and brought to Cerimon, a lord
whose belief is that "virtue and cunning" are "endowments
greater than nobleness and riches." He admits he has studied
physics,

Through which secret art
By turning o'er authorities, I have
Together with my practice, made familiar
To me and to my aid the blest infusions
That dwell in vegetives, in metals, stones;
And I can speak of the disturbances
That nature works, and of her cures; which doth give me
A more content in course of delight
Than to be thirsty after tottering honour,
Or tie my treasure up in silken bags,
To please the fool and death.

(III, ii, 32–42)

Cerimon who professes honesty and humility in the study of books about his art, also shares Friar Laurence's high regard for plants, metals, and stones. As a healer, he brings honor, charity, and knowledge to aid his patients to health.

Cerimon orders the coffin opened and discovers inside a scroll that identifies the apparently lifeless Thaisa as Pericles' queen and requests her burial by the finder. Cerimon detects a "delicate odour" from the coffin, and, noticing her lifelike appearance, orders a fire and boxes of medicine from his closet so that he may try to revive her.

I heard of an Egyptian
That had nine hours lien dead,
Who was by good appliance recovered.

(III, ii, 84–86)

The mention of Egypt would be significant to anyone in the audience familiar with the sources of magic. As Cerimon resuscitates her, a bystander implies that he has received his powers from heaven, suggesting thereby the tradition of the white magician. In the manner of the Doctor in *King Lear* (IV, vii, 24), Cerimon also calls for music to aid his cure. As he carries her away, successful in his task, he begs Aesculepius, the god of medicine, to guide him in his work.

Another cure, this time of a King, is a focal point of

All's Well That Ends Well.[14] Helena, who is the orphaned daughter of the late Gerard de Narbonne, a celebrated physician, endeavors to rid the King of France of a fistula. Enamored of the noble Bertram, she hopes to win his hand by curing the King with her father's "prescriptions of rare and proved effects" (I, iii, 227-28). She follows Bertram from Rousillon to the court at Paris, where she gains audience with the King, who assures her that he is incurable: "our most learned doctors" and "the congregated college have concluded that labouring art can never ransome nature from her inaidable estate" (II, i, 120-21). Helena convinces the despairing King that she is not an imposter and demonstrates her confidence by asserting that should her cure prove unsuccessful, "with vilest torture let my life be ended" (II, i, 177). Balancing her life upon the outcome, Helena extracts the promise of an unnamed reward. When she completes the cure within her brief, stipulated time limit, Lafeu, an old courtier, implies that the court should be in awe of her wonder-working. His attitude summarizes the ambivalences of a world increasingly aware of the effects of empirical proof but still able to believe in the power of miracles. Lafeu concludes that Helena's gifts supersede those of both Paracelsus and Galen. There is no detailed account of the cure,[15] but the audience is left with the impression that it was both miraculous and magical. Possibly Helena's deceased father, Gerard de Narbonne, had been a white magician and his "prescriptions" were still effective in her hands.

---

14. See W. W. Lawrence, *Shakespeare's Problem Comedies* (New York, 1931), pp. 32-37, for the two stories that Shakespeare took from Boccaccio for this play; only the first of these is pertinent here.

15. *The Secretes of the Reverend Maister Alexis, of Piemont* (London, 1580), p. 11. For curing a fistula (such as the King's) this book recommends: "Make oyle of Brimstone, to heal all manners of cankers, diseases, or sores, which come of a putrified humour, and runne continually, commonly calles Fistules." There is also a recipe offered for the cure-all elixir of life: "Dissolve and reduce golde into a potable licour, which conserveth the youth and healthe of a man, and will heale every . . . disease that is thought incurable, in the space of seven daies at the furthest."

Though hardly a white magician herself, Paulina, in the last act of *The Winter's Tale,* does display some of the magician's outward trappings. Not only is she the agent who manipulates the restoration of Hermione to the repentant Leontes, but her means of presenting the queen as a statue is suggestive of the white magician's task of infusing powers and life into statues he has created. Moreover, the ceremony is accompanied by music, as is Thaisa's "rebirth."

Admiring the statue, Leontes says: "There's magic in thy majesty." And as Hermione walks from her pedestal to "strike all that look upon with marvel," Paulina reassures her audience that "her actions shall be holy as you hear my spell is lawful." Leontes finally affirms the aura of magic that has permeated the encounter when he embraces Hermione:

> O, she's warm!
> If this be magic, let it be an art
> Lawful as eating.
> (V, iii, 109–11)

By emphasizing the lawfulness of magic, Shakespeare asks the audience to accept the whole ceremony as if it were created solely for a benevolent reunion.

Healing maladies by touch, a technique in use since before Christ, was another power claimed by healers in Shakespeare's time, and, in earlier days, by some English kings. Edward the Confessor was believed to have possessed the skill to rid suppliants of the king's evil, or scrofula. Needless to say, contemporary physicians diplomatically did not question this wonder-working. Shakespeare puts this legend to use in *Macbeth,* when Malcolm and Macduff, planning to return to Scotland to defeat Macbeth are told by a doctor of the English King's royal touch. Malcolm develops this theme:

> 'Tis call'd the evil:

A most miraculous work in this good king:
Which often, since my here-remain in England,
I have seen him do. How he solicits heaven,
Himself best knows: but strangely-visited people,
All swoln and ulcerous, pitiful to the eye,
The mere despair of surgery, he cures,
Hanging a golden stamp about their necks,
Put on with holy prayers: and 'tis spoken,
To the succeeding royalty he leaves
The healing benediction. With this strange virtue,
He hath a heavenly gift of prophecy,
And sundry blessings hang about his throne,
That speak him full of grace.

(IV, iii, 143–59)

No doubt Shakespeare pleased King James with this passage, for in 1605 James claimed he had the divine right of the royal touch. But of course the passage is also essential to the play, the beneficent effects of the touch serving as a direct contrast to the plague of evil that Macbeth has visited upon Scotland.

Despite these appearances of the healer, Shakespeare does not usually provide any detail about white magic and rarely mentions the specific handling of properties that effect cures. Nor does he introduce any elaborate magical rite. Not to be confused with the physicians of Elizabethan drama or those merely present to administer poisons in court intrigues,[16] his figures are, instead, agents who assume the roles of priest, doctor, and wonder-worker. They emerge as benevolently dedicated to the task of aiding society for its own good; they also can be used by the playwright for the purposes of romantic comedy, where reconciliation and final harmony are keynotes. Healing through the art of white magic, moreover, brings natural order to the physical

---

16. See Kenneth Koch's M.A. thesis, "The Physician in English Drama," Columbia University, 1953; also John Moyes, *Medicine and Kindred Arts in the Plays of Shakespeare* (Glasgow, 1896).

body, just as it can bring health and good government to the disordered body politic. Since life in the Renaissance was dependent on both a healthy body and a healthy state, if healing worked, all was well; if it failed, the consequences were worse disorder.

4

Antecedents of *The Tempest*

*A*t a time when the human body was readily subject to
plague and disease and the English body politic
was still vulnerable, either to insurrection or the threat of
Spanish invasion, the possibilities of achieving order through
the aids of white magic were strongly appealing to audiences.
Just as healing through white magic was shown to bring
health to the diseased individual, so it might also promote
order in the diseased body politic. The traditional white
magician might conduct his benevolent works either to cure
the individual through herbs at an auspicious astrological
moment, or, on a far more overreaching scale, to reconcile
rebels or usurpers and thus bring order to a foundering
state.

Through such insights a few might have identified Prospero. As a figure of far wider faculties than the healers of
the previous chapter, and undoubtedly the major white
magician in English Renaissance drama, his relationship
to healing and order is based upon the interconnection of
art and nature: to effect reconciliation, he evokes the assis-

tance of the hidden properties of nature and then governs them through his magical art. Prospero's power over his spirit Ariel enables him to accomplish a series of triumphant maneuvers that culminate in a harmonious reunion as well as in his restoration to a usurped throne. Not only does he cure some of the diseased minds of the rebels but he also cures the diseased body politic of his kingdom. Once he has achieved these benevolent ends, he abandons celestial aid and resumes his earthly rights as a mortal.

Undoubtedly the response of an early seventeenth-century audience to Prospero's white magic would have partially depended upon its knowledge of similar characters in earlier plays, whether they be enchanters, gods, fairies, magicians, princely exiles, or hermits. To better assess what such an understanding may have been, and before more fully dissecting the magical acts of Prospero, it will be worthwhile first to examine a sampling of other figures in contemporary drama whose relationship to white magic is also significant, and to look as well at a few magicians whom some critics claim to have been archetypes for Prospero. Clearly these are not black magicians like Doctor Faustus, or Peter Fabell in *The Merry Devil of Edmonton* (1602), or Alexander Borgia in *The Devil's Charter* (1607): white magicians were never ambitious, covetous, or willing to barter their souls with the Devil. Nor are they similar to such witches as Medusa in *Fedele and Fortunio* (*Two Italian Gentlemen*) (1584), Joan La Pucelle in *Henry VI,* Part I (1592), or Erichto (from Lucan) in *The Tragedie of Sophonisba* (1605).

There are, however, a few enchanters who are hardly beneficent but still are not specifically allied with evil forces. Such a figure is Friar Camolet in Chapman's *Bussy D'Ambois* (1604). He is far from saintly in aiding the adultery of Tamyra and Bussy, though, to the sure, they are the play's romantic protagonists. And he does raise devils, not Neoplatonic daemons, in his effort to gain foreknowledge over Bussy's enemies. His magic, moreover, does nothing to halt Bussy's downfall and works mostly as a dramatic device for spectacle.

Most frequently the enchanter leans upon magic as a means of seduction and amorous gain, only to experience ephemeral triumph and ignominious defeat. The humorous coward, Bryan Sans Foy, in *Sir Clyomen and Sir Clamydes* (1570), strives to secure the hand of Juliana, Princess of Denmark, through fulfilling her condition for a husband: the delivery to her of the head of the flying serpent, who lives in the Wood of Marvels on a diet of humans. Bryan Sans Foy inveigles Sir Clamydes into the valiant task of severing the monster's head; then he magically induces sleep in the true victor while claiming Juliana as his own prize. Waking too soon, however, Sir Clamydes unmasks the enchanter's deceptive trick.

Likewise, Sacrapant in George Peele's *The Old Wives Tale* (1590) employs magic to seduce: disguising himself as a dragon that he may ensnare Delia, he announces arrogantly that he will never die except "by a dead man's hand." All too soon, this unlikely "divination" is born out: his ambitious life ends at the hands of an apparition, Jack the Ghost.

Outwitted also is the Enchanter in *The Wisdome of Dr. Dodypoll* (1599), who, attracted by Lucilia, entices her from her betrothed through magic. Lucilia's father, however, possesses a ring that contains magical virtues, and, in what approximates an act of white magic, overcomes the Enchanter and puts him to flight.[1]

Defeat also awaits the enchantress whose magic leads to seduction: Amaryllis, in Fletcher's *The Faithful Shepherdess* (1608-1609), employs a charm learned from her grandmother in an attempt to seduce Perigot and to destroy his love for the chaste Amoret. With the help of the Sullen

---

1. This version of the delivery of a maid from an enchanter may have influenced the plot of Milton's *Comus*.

Shepherd, she has herself transformed into the likeness of Amoret by a combination of herbs, words, and a dunking in the holy well. Although her activities nearly lead to Amoret's death, Amaryllis cannot be considered a black magician or evil witch so much as a misguided person in whom power has been misplaced. Clorin, acting as healer, brings about a happy ending for the chaste lovers.

Except for Lucilia's father, none of the enchanters possesses the attributes of white magicians. Temporary victories are the lot of the enchanter, who, as will become clear in a following chapter, repeatedly takes the role of adversary in the court masque. There he is pitted against a god whose powers may be infinite but also invite comparison with those of Prospero. Gods as protagonists, moreover, do appear in plays as well as court masques: for instance, the goddesses Venus and Fortune each believes herself of greater usefulness to mankind in *The Rare Triumphs of Love and Fortune* (1582), and their mutual challenge suggests overtones of the magicians' contest. When Mercury strikes "with his Rod three times" to conjure up the souls of such worthies as Troilus and Cressida, Alexander, Dido, and Hero and Leander, all report on the relative merits of the two goddesses. In addition, the goddesses follow the trials of the true lovers—Hermione, the man, and Fidelia, daughter of the King.

Having escaped from court on learning that Fidelia's suspicious brother Armenio intends to separate them, they are guided by Hermione's long-lost father, Bomelio, who, years earlier, was unjustly exiled from the court because of his "fawning freends." Bomelio, whose magicianship cannot be classed as purely white, calls upon the "fury" Tisiphone, as well as other demons, to wreak vengeance on his enemies and strike Armenio dumb. It is this same Bomelio who was cited in chapter 2 as an example of magicians whose books were burned, for his son Hermione destroys the books in horror on discovering their content. Bomelio goes mad as a result, but Mercury charms him to sleep and, as an all-powerful healer, takes some drops of blood from Fidelia to effect his cure. Fortune announces to the King the gods' remedy for Armenio's dumbness—a magical ceremony, after which Armenio can speak, the lovers are united, and Bomelio regains his senses, to be accepted at the court once again. Venus claims the victory of reconciliation, but, not to be outdone, Fortune announces that wisdom is the true winner of their contest.

Between the gods and the white magician in the scale of supernatural power stands Oberon, King of the Fairies, who appears first in *The Scottish History of James the Fourth* (1590-1591) of Robert Greene, and later in Shakespeare's *A Midsummer Night's Dream* (*c.* 1591-1596). In the former play, Oberon appears primarily in the induction or frame-story and in the choruses between the acts, although he does step into the main action to rescue a character in the last act. Shakespeare's Oberon confines his supernatural acts almost wholly to administering a love potion and its antidote, both to humans and to his fairy wife. He acts through his servant Puck, who behaves somewhat like a familiar spirit, even though Oberon, not being a human magician, has no logical need for such service and could presumably act directly without using Puck if he chose to do so. Oberon's interference in human affairs is almost consistently benevolent, except for his share in the temporary transformation of Bottom the Weaver. His actions within Fairyland and his relationship with Titania are perhaps beyond the judgment of mortals. Study and dedication are not expected of gods or fairies, but Oberon's guidance of Puck shows a fatherly concern for his moral improvement not unlike that of a magician for his apprentice; this trait is even more pronounced in the prose tale *The Mad Pranks and Merry Jests of Robin Goodfellow* (before 1588).[2]

2. Cf. Robert Reed, *The Occult on the Tudor and Stuart Stage* (Boston, 1965), pp. 196–200.

On the plane of mortals, Friar Bacon, whose participation in a contest and whose renunciation of magic have also been discussed in chapter 2, reveals elements both of black and of white magic in his activities in Greene's *Friar Bacon and Friar Bungay* (1589). Although Bacon has no written compact with the Devil, he does seek out devils and refers to his magic as "nigromantic skill." With some vanity, he boasts of his theatrical deeds: the magician contest with Vandermast; the Brazen head experiment and Bacon's patriotic wall of brass; and the act of rendering useless the swords of Prince Edward and his party. Although some of his methods are questionable, most of Bacon's aims are benevolent. His love for England is evident, and for a moment he takes on the cast of a true white magician as he predicts that all "shall stoop and wonder at Diana's rose." This prediction of glory for the Tudor rose of Elizabeth is the outcome of study and prayerful dedication, a fundamental aspect of white magic. Its message to the audience affirms a continuance of England's peace and prosperity.

The hero Aramanthus, like Prospero and other princes in romantic comedy, is exiled in *The Mayde's Metamorphosis* (1600). Living as a hermit magician, he unites Ascanio, the son of the Duke, and Eurymine, daughter of the Duke's enemy. As a shepherdess, Eurymine takes refuge in the woods, where, to avoid the approaches of Apollo, she requests the god himself to change her "from shape of mayd to man," which, remarkably enough, he does.

Later in the play, Aramanthus asks some Muses to beg Apollo to change her to a "mayd" once more. Touched by the plea, the god brings Ascanio and Eurymine together in marriage and reinstates Aramanthus, revealing him to be the long-lost father of the girl. As such, he shares with Prospero the punishment of exile and a characteristic sympathy for young lovers, one of whom turns out to be his daughter. Bomelio of *The Rare Triumphs of Love and Fortune* was also seen to be another such exile who promotes marriage between his son and the daughter of his enemy, the King.

Indeed, many other plays and stories dating from the same period as *The Tempest* share plot elements with it. Without stirring what Kermode refers to as a "prize mare's nest" of "Bulgarian, Byzantine, Latin, Italian, Spanish, and German testimony"[3] in a search for the source of *The Tempest,* we can discuss a few German, Spanish, and Italian works as "analogous literature," noting particularly the magical acts and character traits identifiable with Prospero.

Ayrer's play, *Die Schöne Sidea,* initially appears to contain striking resemblances to *The Tempest.* Sidea's father is an exiled magician; he captures the son of his enemy by a charm which makes him unable to draw his sword; he puts him to work carrying wood under Sidea's supervision; Sidea falls in love with this prince, Engelbrecht; and the play concludes with their marriage and the reinstatement of the magician-prince. Yet, despite these similarities, the dissimilarities are even more striking. The magician-prince Ludolff is nothing like Prospero; Ludolff is deposed partly because he has killed his enemy's envoy, so his cause is not so clearly just as Prospero's. He is aided not by a spirit like Ariel but by the devil Runzifall, and he does everything in his power to prevent the union between Sidea and Engelbrecht.

Albert Cohn sees a resemblance between the devil Runzifall and Caliban, "who indeed is not the evil one himself but one of his progeny."[4] But Runzifall's functions are more like Ariel's; Caliban never performs supernatural feats for Prospero. Another character in *Sidea* has more in common with Caliban: John Molitor the Miller, who shows himself in the subplot to be lustful and untrustworthy. But, for a moment Molitor also resembles Ariel. As he plays on his

---

3. William Shakespeare, *The Tempest,* ed. Frank Kermode (New York, 1954), lxvi.

4. Albert Cohn, *Shakespeare in Germany in the Sixteenth and Seventeenth Centuries: An Account of English Actors in Germany and the Netherlands and of the Plays Performed by Them During the Same Period* (London, 1865), lxx.

whistle and drums "the devil dances," say the stage directions, and "other devils appear, who all dance too. At last John leaves off."[5] None of this, however, is instigated by Ludolff, who is very angry at the distraction.

At the same time, Sidea, unlike Miranda, has a wand of her own, and uses it to strike Runzifall temporarily dumb when she and Engelbrecht escape. She is also able to restore Engelbrecht's memory by giving him a potion near the close of the play when he has forgotten her and is about to marry another girl.

The fairy-tale aspect of the play, Kermode and others believe, is a clue to the resemblances between *The Tempest* and *Sidea:* "Ultimately the source of *The Tempest* is an ancient *motif,* of almost universal occurrence, in saga, ballad, fairy tale and folk tale. The existence of this story accounts for the many analogues to *The Tempest.* That both Prospero and the father of Ayrer's Sidea are irascible is, in the last analysis, explained by the fact that they descend from a bad-tempered giant magician."[6]

Apparently, Prospero is even further removed from these fairy-tale magicians than he is from Ludolff. The archetypal magician is seldom a human being: in the tale "Lady Featherflight," he is a cannibal-giant, and in the related Italian tale, "La Paloma," it is the girl's mother, an ogress, who captures the prince.[7] The prince in this story finds himself rooted to the spot when he tries to draw his sword, and later is given tasks to perform, including splitting each of six cords of wood into four.

Somewhat more like Prospero than Ludolff is Dardanus, the dethroned magician-king of the fourth chapter of Antonio de Eslava's *Noches de Invierno* (1609). When his daughter Seraphina is ready to take a husband, he captures for her the elder son of his enemy and brings him to a

---

5. *Ibid.,* col. 54.
6. Kermode, lxiii.
7. W. W. Newell, "Sources of Shakespeare's *Tempest,*" *Journal of American Folklore* 16 (1903):240, 244.

magical submarine palace where they all live in exile. He also raises a storm to catch the usurping younger brother of his new son-in-law, Valentinian. In the end, he returns to his former kingdom but abdicates in favor of Valentinian and Seraphina.[8]

Another magician who captures a husband for his daughter appears in one of the stories of Calahorra's *Espejo de Principes y Caballeros* (1602; translated later). Other parts of the book contain further magicians, several storms, and a Caliban-like character named Fauno, son of a devil-worshiping mother and possessor of the "Island of the Demoniac."[9]

Finally, there are the numerous magicians of the pastorals of the Italian Commedia dell'Arte. These do not resemble Prospero in character so much as the various pastoral scenarios resemble *The Tempest* in plot elements.[10]

---

8. Joseph de Perott, *The Probable Source of the Plot of Shakespeare's Tempest* (Worcester, Mass., 1905), p. 214.
9. *Ibid.*
10. K. M. Lea, *Italian Popular Comedy: a Study in the Commedia dell'-Arte, 1560–1620, with Special Reference to the English Stage* (Oxford, 1934), 1:201–3. Miss Lea has assembled a typical scenario by choosing incidents from a number of such pastorals. She claims that the
> three sources of dramatic interest in the pastorals of the Commedia dell'Arte are the love affairs of the natives of Arcadia, the power of the Magician, and the horse-play of shipwrecked buffoons.

5

Prospero
as the White Magician

*C*learly, the sources that could have affected Shake-speare in his creation of Prospero are innumerable. In writing *The Tempest,* he may have assumed that not only had much of his audience already been introduced to various magician figures in earlier plays, but also that some might even be familiar with some of the magician plays and stories from the Continent. Aware of the Church's opposition to all forms of magic, exposed to plays, stories, folk and fairy tales, and, in some cases, to the more specialized and covert magical writings, most audiences possessed such a truly commonplace knowledge of magic, both black and white, that a popular response to Prospero as a white magician was assured. With this view in mind, we shall examine Prospero and his art, an art that allows him to perform miraculous operations over nature by enlisting the aid of the "intelligences of heaven."

Applying his cultivated knowledge to control the continually erupting possibilities of black magic, Prospero struggles to maintain white magic's supremacy. At the outset of the play, he has already suppressed and enslaved Caliban, who, as the offspring of the Devil and the witch Sycorax, is inevitably deformed. Such a clash between the cultivated and the uncouth is common in the tradition of white magic, so common in fact that Kermode believes the play's chief crisis hinges upon the conflict between the Art of Prospero and the Nature of Caliban.[1]

Between the polarities of black and white magic lie the universal realities and the problems of life that also exist outside the enchanted island. The chaotic lives of Prospero's enemies require order, purification, and some of the self-discipline that Prospero has learned in the study of white magic. Only then may they receive the knowledge he offers them and acquire virtue. At the beginning of the play, greed, lust, and ambition permeate their behavior: Alonso has usurped Prospero's throne; Antonio and Sebastian plot murder; and Stephano and Trinculo, attracting Caliban as their ally, stumble toward a vision of power through murder.

Prospero is effective in his task to the extent that he illuminates a self-awareness within the island's visitors, some of whom are then able, through repentance, to find a state of grace and reordered lives. His forgiveness completes their "sea-change" and readies them to participate in a beneficial reunion.[2]

Through his art, Prospero has for some time been free from the destructive passions that have hold of his enemies. His study and reflection have led him to "an ordination of civility, the control of appetite, the transformation of nature by breeding and learning; . . . the means of Grace," all of which qualities suggest the development of the white magi-

---

1. William Shakespeare, *The Tempest,* ed. Frank Kermode, *Arden Shakespeare,* rev. ed. (Cambridge, Mass., 1954), p. xxiv.
2. See R. G. Hunter, *Shakespeare and the Comedy of Forgiveness* (New York, 1965), pp. 239–41.

cian.[3] Certainly Prospero reveals no interest in gaining the universal domination of a Faustus, nor does he seek out other magicians merely to test his own power. His full-fledged skills serve largely to gain his rightful ascendancy to his own kingdom. He achieves his goals through an awareness of past, present, and future, trusting his foreknowledge as a guide to take his enemies into his power and bring fresh order into their lives.[4] Astrologically, he assesses the timing of their arrival on the island as an act of "bountiful Fortune":

> I find my zenith doth depend upon
> A most auspicious star, whose influence
> If now I court not, but omit, my fortunes
> Will ever after droop.
>
> (I, i, 180–84)

His wish is for the safety and protection of those who unwittingly participate in his magical exercise; and of his tempest, he informs Miranda,

> I have with such provision in mine Art
> So safely ordered, that there is no soul—
> No, not so much perdition as an hair
> Betid to any creature in the vessel
> Which thou heard'st cry, which thou saw'st sink.
>
> (I, ii, 28–32)

Not only does he tell Miranda that none in the shipwreck has been harmed, but also that he has "done nothing but in care of" her. In questioning Ariel later, his first concern after quelling the storm is for the safety of the shipwrecked. He learns that,

> not a hair perish'd;
> On their sustaining garments not a blemish,

---

3. Kermode, p. xlviii.
4. Rose Abdelnour Zimbardo, "Form and Disorder in *The Tempest*," *Shakespeare Quarterly* 14 (1963) :49–56.

But fresher than before. . . .
                                    (I, ii, 217–19)

Ariel adds that the King's ship is safely harbored "in the deep nook, where once thou call'dst me up at midnight to fetch dew from the still-vex'd Bermoothes." Later, the Boatswain amazedly reports that their ship "is light and yare and bravely rigg'd, as when we first put out to sea." Gonzalo, who had originally saved the lives of Prospero and Miranda, judges their survival from the tempest to be a "miracle" and a rare phenomenon:

> That our garments, being, as they were,
> drenched in the sea, hold, not withstanding,
> their freshness and glosses, being rather new-
> dyed than stained with salt-water.
>   (II, i, 58–62)

Not forgetting his daughter, Prospero also extends his protective overwatching to the burgeoning relationship between Miranda and Ferdinand:

> Heavens rain grace
> On that which breeds between 'em.
>   (III, i, 75–76)

Prospero's actions parallel some of the criteria of Agrippa, who recommends that "the tradition of Magicall art rightfully and lawfully prepared" is essential to the practice of white magic and entails consecration of books and study.[5] Prospero indeed claims to Miranda that in Milan he was "in dignity, and for the liberal Arts without a parallel." "Rapt in secret studies," he dedicated himself to the bettering of his mind: "my library was dukedom large enough."[6] On immersing himself in these books, however,

---

5. Agrippa, *Three Books of Occult Philosophy,* trans. J. F. (London, 1651), III, lxii, 540.

6. See James E. Philips, "*The Tempest* and the Renaissance Idea of Man," *SQ* 15 (1964):ii, 147–59. Philips equates Caliban with the vegetative soul, Ariel the sensitive soul, and Prospero the rational soul, which is sustained

he relinquished his temporal ducal power to his brother, whose machinations he could not then overcome. Exiled and set adrift at sea, he eventually landed on the enchanted island. There the knowledge he has acquired and the magical powers he has gained finally come to fruition. How well these books aid Prospero Caliban apparently knows, for later, conspiring with Stephano and Trinculo against his master, he advises them:

> Remember
> First to possess his books: for without them
> He's but a sot, as I am, nor hath not
> One spirit to command. . . .
>   (III, ii, 89–92)

When finally he abjures his Art, Prospero leaves to last of all, the disposal of his books.

Agrippa also emphasizes the need in white magic for "the vertue of the person himself consecrating" and "his holiness of life," and Prospero suitably exhibits the virtues of piety, temperance, and discipline.[7] Righteous anger does break through, however, as he anticipates confronting the conspirators, who remind him of his usurped throne in Milan as well as of the conspiracies of Caliban, Antonio, and Sebastian. At the wedding masque, Miranda confides in Ferdinand that

> Never till this day,
> Saw I him touch'd with anger, so distemper'd.
>   (IV, i, 144–45)

Prospero himself asks his future son-in-law to

> Bear with my weakness; my old brain is troubled:
> Be not disturb'd with my infirmity:
> If you be pleas'd retire into my cell,

---

by the vegetative and served by the sensitive souls. Prospero's learning brings with it self-knowledge and the education of his rational soul.

7. Agrippa, III, lxii, 540.

> And there repose: a turn or two I'll walk,
> To still by beating mind.
>
> (IV, i, 159–63)

In the end, it is Ariel's compassionate feeling for Prospero's enemies that moves the magician to relinquish his anger and find forgiveness. As spirits were believed not to have feelings, Ariel's pleading is indeed cogent, and Prospero responds to it:

> Hast thou, which art but air, a touch, a feeling
> Of their afflictions, and shall not myself,
> One of their kind, that relish all as sharply
> Passion as they, be kindlier moved than thou art?
> Though with their high wrongs I am struck to th' quick,
> Yet with my nobler reason 'gainst my fury
> Do I take part: the rarer action is
> In virtue than in vengeance: they being penitent,
> The sole drift of my purpose doth extend
> Not a frown further.
>
> (V, i, 21–30)

His dedication to white magic does not permit Prospero to lose control of his passions for long, and, after all, he is "schoolmaster" to Miranda and disciplinarian to both Ariel and Caliban. His skill in white magic is not only more potent than the black magic of Sycorax, who "could contract the moon, make flows and ebbs," but, according to her son, Caliban, even more so than that of her god:

> His Art is of such pow'r
> It would control my dam's god, Setebos,
> And make a vassal of him.
>
> (I, ii, 374–76)

As a witch or black magician, Sycorax might have used many of the properties available to the white magician, but the sphere of her command encompassed only devils and lesser spirits. These lacked the potency of the Neoplatonic daemons available to Prospero: his spirits proved more effective because they were hierarchically closer to God.

With such spirits watching over Prospero, Caliban's curses, pale images of his mother's black-magical invocations, are powerless. They only provoke Prospero to send cramps, sidestitches, and urchins to plague Caliban, who is "pinch'd as thick as honeycomb, each pinch more stinging than bees that made 'em." (In the sixteenth century, fairies were believed to pinch those with whom they were displeased.[8]) As a punishment to the participants in Caliban's conspiracy, Prospero orders goblins to "grind their joints with dry convulsions; shorten up their sinews with aged cramps. . . ."

Caliban complains that Prospero's spirits hear and watch him, setting upon him "for every trifle," whenever the magician commands. These spirits, "meaner" than Ariel, metamorphose into apes, hedgehogs, and adders, and attack Caliban so frequently that he even mistakes Trinculo for some fresh devil or monster bent upon tormenting him.[9]

His master characterizes Caliban as a creature, "on whose nature nurture can never stick," "a freckled whelp, hagborn," "a mis-shapen knave" situated well below the level of man. And most significantly he calls him a "devil, a born devil," just as he accuses the royal conspirators of being "worse than devils." In the white magical setting of the

---

8. Minor Latham, *The Elizabethan Fairies* (New York, 1930), pp. 26, 180–81; and see K. M. Briggs, *The Anatomy of Puck* (London, 1959). Many Elizabethans believed that fairies were their neighbors. There were at least two varieties. One depended upon mortals for domestic supplies, meting out reward or physical punishment, depending on the extent of human aid they received. These were either fallen angels or creatures inhabiting a middle ground between heaven and hell, and they were tyrannical, perhaps like the lesser spirits that Ariel commands for Prospero. The other variety, however was diminutive and an outgrowth of Shakespeare's invention, the good fairies of *A Midsummer Night's Dream*. This is the Ariel who sings: "In a cowslip bell I lie."

9. Caliban is not alone in mistaking a human for a spirit. Miranda mistakes Ferdinand for one at their initial encounter (I, ii, 413–14); later, Ferdinand accurately identifies spirits in the masque, and Prospero confirms that they are

> Spirits, which by mine Art
> I have from their confines call'd to enact
> My present fancies.
>
> (IV, i, 120-22)

play, where Prospero employs Neoplatonic daemons and spirits, this designation places all the conspirators in the sphere of Sycorax and the devils of black magic.

Above them and above Prospero, somewhere between man and angel, lives Ariel, a neutral, rational Neoplatonic spirit. Without him Prospero could have accomplished little. Not so rebellious as Lucifer, and not used by Shakespeare as a fallen angel, Ariel does belong partially to that disobedient band that God expelled from heaven.[10] Such fallen angels, however, were still superior to rational man, shaping man's destiny and salvation, moving and creating anything with immediate dispatch, and directing every phase of man's perceptions.[11] Kermode rightly follows Curry in believing Ariel to have the qualities of the "intelligences" of medieval theology, qualities that include such characteristics as

> simultaneous knowledge of all that happens; understanding of the cause of things; the power to alter his position in space in no time, and to manipulate the operations of nature, so as, for example, to create tempests; the power to work upon a human being's will and imagination for good or evil ends; and total invulnerability to assault by material instruments.[12]

Enacting his charge at his master's command, Ariel uses independent judgment to choose what powers to enforce. If he requires lesser and irrational spirits to aid his tasks, he controls them through his superior strength. Both he and they become "ministers of Fate" to all those on the island who undergo a "sea-change."

As a pure intelligence, Ariel has the capacity to exist interchangeably, as need be, in each of the four elements,

> be't to fly
> To swim, to dive into the fire, to ride
> On the curl'd clouds.
>   (I, i, 190–92)

---

10. See C. S. Lewis, *The Discarded Image* (Cambridge, 1964), pp. 134–38.
11. Walter Clyde Curry, *Shakespeare's Philosophical Patterns* (Baton Rouge, 1937), pp. 141–59.
12. Kermode, p. 143.

At one moment Prospero commands him

> to tread the ooze of the salt deep,
> To run upon the sharp wind of the north,
> To do me business in the veins o' th' earth
> When it is bak'd with frost.
>
> (I, ii, 253–56)

At another time, after the shipwreck, Ariel reports how he "flam'd amazement" to "burn in many places." While conducting Ferdinand through the isle, he is disguised as a "nymph o' th' sea," "invisible to every eyeball" save Prospero's. At the mock banquet, he appears "like a Harpy." Clearly, Ariel's ability instantly to metamorphose both shape and disguise is infinite.

The meaner spirits share Ariel's fluidity, appearing as "several strange Shapes, bringing in a banquet"; as nymphs and reapers at the wedding masque; or as "divers Spirits, in shape of dogs and hounds," pursuing Caliban's party. In every case, however, they take their orders through Ariel, the master spirit. With Ariel, they, too, eventually receive their liberty, since, according to tradition, spirits gave their services only grudgingly, after considerable coaxing by the magician.

From the outset of the play, in fact, Ariel demands his liberty, receiving rebuffs from his master, who reminds him of "the foul witch Sycorax," who confined him within a pine tree for "refusing her grand hests." Of course, Prospero can command Ariel even against his will because he has a greater affinity to him than did Sycorax, who lacked such power and could only invoke and imprison him. Aware of Prospero's greater magic, Ariel fulfills each task instantly and with complete obedience:

> I will be correspondent to command
> And so my spiriting gently.
>
> (I, ii, 296–97)

When summoned, "Come with a thought," Ariel is there;
and later, at another task, Ariel cries,

> I drink the air before me, and return
> Or ere your pulse twice beat.
>
> (V, i, 102–3)

Following the tempest, Ariel demonstrates his versatility
and power by leading Ferdinand to Miranda, disrupting
both the royal and the Caliban conspiracies, and finally
conducting the conspirators to his master. Responding with
gratitude, Prospero fondly promises that Ariel will be "free
as mountain winds," upon all human departure from the
island.

Until that time, his magical means for luring the various
parties to their destinies about the island is music.[13] Through
it, the spellbound, as Ferdinand relates, regain their senses:

> This music crept by me upon the waters,
> Allaying both their fury and my passion
> With its sweet air: thence I have followed it,
> Or it hath drawn me rather.
>
> (I, ii, 394–98)

Since while he is singing Ariel is invisible to all save Prospero, Ferdinand is bewildered about whether the sound is
"'i' th' air or the 'arth":

> This is no mortal business, nor no sound
> That the earth owes.
>
> (I, ii, 409–10)

When the royal party hears Ariel play "solemn music," all
save the two conspirators are struck immediately by a
"strange drowsiness." Through his skill and prescience of

---

13. G. Wilson Knight, *The Shakespearean Tempest* (London, 1953),
pp. 247–66. Knight believes in a tempest-music opposition at work throughout the play, a structure of "sea grief and final love and union or reunion,"
overlaid by the harmonies of music, "as mankind finds repentance and
recognition."

the burgeoning conspiracy, Prospero guides Ariel to awaken
Gonzalo with a song: "Shake off slumber and beware."

Though unconscious of its magical properties, Caliban
relates that the music does not harm but rather induces
sleep and visions:[14]

> Be not afeard; the isle is full of noises,
> Sounds and sweet airs, that give delight, and hurt not.
> Sometimes a thousand twangling instruments
> Will hum about mine ears; and sometime voices,
> That, if I then had wak'd after long sleep,
> Will make me sleep again: and then, in dreaming
> The clouds methought would open, and show riches
> Ready to drop upon me, that, when I wak'd
> I cried to dream again.[15]
>
> (III, ii, 133–41)

"Marvellous sweet music" is an integral part of the "excel-
lent dumb discourse" at the mock banquet, and later it
accompanies the masque, which Prospero calls "some vanity
of mine Art."

At other times, magical spells require absolute silence,
as when Prospero orders, "No tongue! all eyes! be silent,"
at the beginning of the masque. At its culmination, he commands Ariel to "hush, and be mute, or else our spell is
marr'd."

Besides the aid of his Neoplatonic daemons, Ariel and
the "meaner spirits," Prospero also wears a magical robe
to supplement his powers. His success in performing each
magical act, in fact, depends upon his wearing of the robe.
At his first appearance, immediately after raising the tem-

---

14. See Northrop Frye, *A Natural Perspective* (New York, 1965), p. 147.
Speaking of Orpheus and the late romances, Frye claims that "Orpheus is
the hero of all four romances, the musical, magical and pastoral power
that awakens Thaisa and Hermione, that draws Ferdinand toward Miranda, that signalizes the ritual death of Imogen and that gives strange
dreams to Caliban."

15. This passage, as well as others in the play, contains imagery of the
masque. It seems likely that Milton was familiar with *The Tempest,* there
being similar types of imagery in *Comus.*

pest, he doffs it ("Lie there, my Art"), but he wears it again later when he magically puts Miranda to sleep and summons Ariel. Shakespeare, moreover, draws particular attention to these "magic robes" in the stage direction at the beginning of Act V, a moment in the play when Prospero uses his magic to bring the separated parties together.

Another crucial part of Prospero's magical equipment is his staff. Unaware of its potency, Ferdinand resists the magician, only to find that "He draws, and is charmed from moving." Instead, Prospero orders him to

> Put thy sword up, traitor;
> Who mak'st a show, but dar'st not strike, thy conscience
> Is so possess'd with guilt: come from thy ward;
> For I can here disarm thee with this stick
> And make thy weapon drop.
>
> (I, ii, 472–76)

This is the staff that Prospero declares he will break and then "bury it certain fadoms in the earth" when he abjures his magic.

Regardless of the instrument he uses, the general effect of all Prospero's magic is temporarily to paralyze his victims and numb their senses:

> Thy nerves are in their infancy again,
> And have no vigour in them,
> (I, ii, 487–88)

he instructs Ferdinand, who then cries, "my spirits, as in a dream, are all bound up." While later, in the feigned banquet scene, Ariel, disguised as a harpy, informs the royal party that they are spellbound. When endeavoring to defend themselves with their swords, Ariel mocks their efforts:

> If you could hurt,
> Your swords are now too massy for your strengths
> And will not be uplifted.
> (III, iii, 66–68)

Returning to his master, Ariel asserts that the royal party are all imprisoned by Prospero's charm,

> In the line-grove which weather-fends your cell;
> They cannot budge till your release.
>
> (V, i, 10–11)

After being lured to the magician, "they all enter the circle which Prospero made, and there stand charm'd." Each has become "spell-stopp'd," his brains "boil'd within" his skull.

To break his charms and restore their senses, Prospero calls upon "heavenly music," hardly the first time that Shakespeare has suggested music's curative powers:

> The charm dissolves apace;
> And as the morning steals upon the night,
> Melting the darkness, so their rising senses
> Begin to chase the ignorant fumes that mantle
> Their clearer reason.
>
> (V, i, 64–68)

Viewing his enemies as penitents (apart from Antonio and Sebastian, whose penitence is ambiguous), Prospero offers them mercy and forgiveness, leading them to a "second life." When embraced by Prospero, Alonso entreats pardon and offers to return the usurped dukedom. As a living consummation of their new-found harmony, Prospero then reveals to the assembly Ferdinand and Miranda, "playing at chess." Through his expertise in white magic, Prospero has reunited his kingdom, healed ancient wounds, and assured future harmony in the union of his daughter and Ferdinand.

At all times do Prospero's actions demonstrate a clear affiliation with white magic: his books, his staff, and his robe are instruments of his calling; his spirits are Neoplatonic daemons and not devils; his magical deeds, although not structured to invoke God, are never atheistic, anti-Christian, or appealing to the Devil. (Only the "Ye elves of hills" speech [V, i, 33-57] overlaps into black magic, being derived from the enchantress Medea's invocation from Ovid's *Metamorphoses*.) Moreover, he enhances his virtue through arduous application, study, and selflessness. The extensive knowledge he gains thereby, together with his human nature and his magic, permit him wisely to conduct the education and self-discovery of all.

Even though Shakespeare elicits sufficient detail only to etch a background of magic to Prospero's acts, white magic functions as a suggestive and pervasive element throughout *The Tempest*. As a symbolic force for good, it becomes in Prospero's hands a crucial instrument for curing the disordered minds of rebels and usurpers as well as the body politic. Within the framework of this late romance, white magic is the protagonist's chief support in his benevolent efforts to vanquish his opposition. As a fundamental plot element of romantic comedy, its effectiveness readily satisfies an audience's inherent need for wish fulfillment. At the same time, white magic heightens dramatic tension, especially for an audience aware of the Church's ban on all varieties of magic. Even though the expectations of a happy outcome in romances and comedies could have allayed such fears, some may still have reacted to Prospero with feelings of apprehension, awe, and helplessness, attributing the terrors of the unknown and the natural calamities of the play to the work of magicians. Others, acquainted with the new science of the early seventeenth century, may have been sceptical. Whichever the view, Prospero belonged as a major protagonist firmly within the tradition of white magic—a tradition inherited from folklore and superstition, from the Church, from popular literature, and from early drama.

6
The Jacobean Court Masque:
The King as White Magician

*A*t the time when the popular open air public theater
of London moved indoors to become more sophisti-
cated and exclusive, the new Jacobean court was allocating
budgets for its own private entertainment that would have
astounded the thrifty Elizabeth. And the budgets grew, for
the masque soon became the most popular courtly diversion,
an extravagant, elaborately-decked, theatrical performance,
usually given no more than once and drawing heavily on
the devices of allegory and mythology. At the core of most
of these masques was the enactment of a symbolic crisis, its
resolution signaling the triumph of virtue, wisdom, and
government over vice, appetite, and disunity.

Although not to the same extent, the masque had also
prospered as an entertainment in the Renaissance courts of
Italy, France, and England. It heightened a special occasion
with art, conscious theatricality, and that most ancient cata-
lyst to magic, wish-fulfillment. It also sanctioned the social

milieu of the court, celebrating the role of kingship with its obligations and the allegiance that the subjects owed it. The courtly participants who stepped into this make-believe world experienced the victory of order over chaos and felt reassured about the stability of their own universe and of the hierarchical society that ruled it. The ceremony that drew the audience into the revels resembled a magical ritual, both audience and masquers entering into a celebration through which nature was controlled and villainous enchanters subdued. At the masque's end, the celebrants emerged optimistically refreshed by the temporary experience of wish-fulfillment and the memory of an insubstantial, idealized vision.

The new century brought with it a crisis in kingship, eventually culminating in the crown's clash with Parliament and the chaos of civil war. Both James I and Charles I precipitated this confrontation by insisting upon their absolute role as king. The masque, of course, reinforced this concept of the king as a symbol of divine power and the giver of fertility and prosperity—the tribal role once filled by the white magician or witch doctor. As the grip of white magic on the public imagination relaxed (the focus on magic shifted to witch trials), the king, as it were, absorbed the role of white magician.

In actuality, neither James nor Charles could exhibit magical powers; yet the masque provided a vehicle to demonstrate their semblance, the nostalgic symbols of the past coalescing in a harmonious synthesis with those of the new age. Despite its sophistication, in fact, the court did not entirely abandon pagan and Platonic traditions, but instead paid respectful lip service to white magic through ancient symbols, while at the same time indulging itself in the uniquely British gift for amateur theatricals. The masque thus became a security fantasy, asserting those very wish-fulfillment elements about the magic of kingly power that were about to be proven untrue. The chaos that the king overcame in the fictional charade of the masque was beyond his control in the new reality of parliamentary Britain.

Such chaos, in several court masques, is due to the willful use of black magic by such enchanters as Circe. Almost invariably, a mythological god or a royal personage to whom the masque pays compliment functions as the victorious adversary of the enchanter and, as an agent in the plot, has the potency of a deus ex machina. His role, in a basic way, is like that of the white magician in Elizabethan plays, the curer of bodily ills as well as ills of the body politic. As the magician must use his magic to try to achieve powers that gods naturally possess, gods are placed at the top of the scale of belief and the white magician toward the bottom. In the middle of this scale are kings, who are already endowed with godlike powers.

The gods within the masque perform acts of magic, retrieving intolerable situations and countering insurmountable forces. Like the king in the reality of his court, they are benefactors, ensuring the survival of society through the deft use of absolute powers. Unlike the white magician, however, they require no magical rites.[1] The goals of the pagan-enchantress on the other hand, are evil. Her charms and spells are largely based upon the manipulation of herbs, a skill that is also the province of the white magician in his role as healer.[2] In the familiar struggle in the masque be-

---

1. Jean Seznec, *The Survival of the Pagan Gods,* trans. Barbara F. Sessions (New York, 1953), pp. 1–83. Although when the masque originated the victors in these masques were pagan mythological gods, they became patrons to groups who euhemeristically saw pagan gods as forerunners of their particular civilizations. Christianity notwithstanding, it was a source of pride to have a mythological ancestor as a benefactor. The pagan gods, moreover, were fully associated with astral bodies, a connection that had prevented their extinction and endowed them with the power of stellar divinities. Mythological gods and astrological magic became inextricable partners, fundamental associates of the magician.

2. See above, chapter 3. In Book XIV of the *Metamorphoses,* Circe is discovered planning to disfigure Scylla with "wicked weedes of grisly jeuce," and later she supervises her ladies and nymphs in the care of her herbs. The charmed potion that she swiftly concocts transforms Ulysses' men to swine, "such force there is in Sorcerie." Only the "peaceprocurer Mercurie,"

tween the chaotic forces of black magic and the harmonious forces of white magic, the deeds of enchanters become more and more spectacular, causing crisis after crisis until finally a climactic act of god, king, or white magician restores harmony and order. Because the concept of chaos and its victorious suppression prove to be most fertile in the masque, some of the different forms this takes are worth inspection.

The archetypal masque to contain such an opposition and contest was *Circe,* or the *Ballet comique de la reine* (1581), where Circe's spell induces chaos and she paralyzes her prisoners. Possibly the most influential masque up to this time, it was remarkable for its clever blending of song, speech, and dance, having more cohesion and sophistication than most similar entertainments that preceded it. At the original performance, indicating the importance of court involvement, the wife of Henry III, Louise of Lorraine, danced to honor his sister's marriage.

The Ballet begins as a gentleman escapes from Circe's palace to plead directly to his sovereign for freedom from captivity. In anger Circe casts a spell on all the dancers that leaves them immobile. Mercury temporarily rescues them through his use of the herb moly, but Circe's ire grows, and she takes everyone prisoner. In opposition, Jupiter, Pan, Minerva, and other assorted divinities mass their forces and jointly attack her palace. Jupiter finally hurls a decisive thunderbolt and Circe capitulates, dutifully allowing herself to be led before the King to do him homage.

What better adversary in the masque, with its aims of testing virtue and affirming harmonious social order, than Circe, who seduces men's wills until they fall to the level of beasts? And what better way to celebrate the King's majesty than to have him foil Circe,[3] for it is with his assistance,

---

protected by the magic plant moly, is able to subdue her. As her bedfellow, he claims a dowry from Circe that enables the men to metamorphose to their original form. See lines 306-13, 345-49, and 417-18.

3. See Dolora Cunningham, "The Jonsonian Masque as a Literary Form," *ELH* 22 (1955):108-24, reprinted in *Ben Jonson, A Collection of Critical Essays* (Englewood Cliffs, N.J., 1960), pp. 160-74.

through his ally Jupiter, a symbolic kinsman, that Circe's dark powers are vanquished and the prisoners of her will restored to freedom?

In William Browne's *Ulysses and Circe* (1615), set on Circe's island, the enchantress appears again, and, of course, is vanquished again. At the outset, and in a speech reminiscent of Medea's Ovidian invocation, a siren reminds us of Circe's formidable feats, declaring that nobody

>   can things begun
> By mighty Circe, daughter to the Sun,
> Check or control; she that by charms can make
> The scaled fish to leave the briny lake,
> And on the seas walk as on land she were;
> She that can pull the pale moon from her sphere,
> And at mid-day the world's all-glorious eye
> Muffle with clouds in long obscurity;
> She that can cold December set on fire,
> And from the grave bodies with life inspire;
> She that can cleave the centre, and with ease
> A prospect make to our Antipodes;
> Whose mystic spells have fearful thunders made,
> And forc'd brave rivers to run retrograde.
> She without storms that sturdy oaks can tear
> And turn their roots where late their curl'd tops were.
> She that can with the winter solstice bring
> All Flora's dainties, Circe, bids me sing;
> And till some greater power her hand can stay,
> Who'er commands, I none but her obey.
>
>   (31–50)[4]

Circe wakes Ulysses from his spellbound sleep and promises to win his love with dance and music. But an antimasque of such creatures as wolves and baboons, in actuality men Circe had transformed, disgusts Ulysses. He reprimands her and Circe relents, surrendering her magical wand to him so that he may awaken his men, still asleep under her spell. As god and white magician Ulysses undoes Circe's

---

4. William Browne, *Poems,* ed. Gordon Goodwin, II (London, 1893), pp. 16–190.

spell and leaves his men free to choose ladies for dancing, at which the Chorus joyously comments:

> And if it lay in Circe's power
> Your bliss might so perserver
> That those you choose but for an hour
> You should enjoy forever.
>
> (318–321)

The status of the enchanter as a figure in the masque appeared to be at its zenith, to judge from the comments of Thomas Campion, in *The Squires' Masque* (1613):

> In ancient times, when any men sought to shadow or heighten his invention, he had store of feigned persons ready for his purpose, as satyrs, nymphs, and their like: such were then in request and belief among the vulgar. But in our days, although they have not utterly lost their use, yet find they so little credit, that our modern writers have rather transferred their fictions to the persons of enchanters and commanders of spirits, as that excellent poet Torquato Tasso hath done, and many others. In imitation of them (having a presentation in hand for persons of high estate) I grounded my whole invention upon enchantments and several transformations.
>
> (1–12)[5]

To precipitate chaos, Campion provided no less than two enchantresses—Error and Rumour—and two enchanters—Curiosity and Credulity. Like the Vice figures of a morality play, they conspire against the squires, so plaguing them with storms on a voyage to England from the Continent[6] that the squires denounce them for "putting all the world into confusion."

A turbulent dance by the four Elements, the four points of the Earth, and the four Winds, symbolizes this chaos. Eternity, "who passes through all enchantments free," ap-

---

5. Thomas Campion, *Poetical Works,* ed. Percival Vivian (London, 1907), pp. 203–14.

6. The masque was presented in the Banqueting Hall at Whitehall in honor of the wedding of the Earl of Somerset to Lady Frances Howard.

pears in "a long blue taffeta robe, painted with stars and on her head a crown." She takes charge, ordering the three Destinies to set before "Bel-Anna," the King's wife, a sacred golden tree:

> Bring away this sacred tree
> The tree of grace and bounty.
> Set it in Bel-Anna's eye,
> For she, she, only she
> Can knotted spells untie.
> Pulled from the stock, let her blest hands carry
> To any suppliant hand a bough,
> And let that hand advance it now
> Against a charm, that charm shall fade away.

The Queen, in what amounts to a ritual act of white magic, plucks a branch from the tree and passes it to the squires, freeing them from the tyranny of enchantment. This signals a fantastic transformation of both scenery and the masquers' attire. As all the participants move forward to the "dancing-place," "London with the Thames is very artificially presented."[7] Fate, Eternity, and the three Destinies may have overcome the men's adversaries, but it is the divine power of the Queen that has the greatest potency for effecting their rescue. Here, the terrestrial personage of the Queen assumes cosmic powers, her dual role as a heavenly and earthly figure stressing again the divine right of kings.

In Jonson's hands the masque reached full maturity, having evolved from episodic speech and debate into a recognized literary genre. Jonson, moreover, altered the form by adding the antimasque, a *concordia discors* device that acted as a counterpoint to the rest of the masque's more dignified and serious content. Parodying the refinements of mythological gods and enchanters with humorous, coarse antics, the antimasquers might dress themselves as animals or witches. When this device first appears in *The Masque*

---

7. Campion, p. 211.

of *Queens* in 1609, Jonson garbs his antimasquers as hags and witches, having them represent such vices as Ignorance, Suspicion, and Credulity—all of which he uses to mock witchcraft.[8] Their leader, The Dame, is yet another enchantress figure, whose invocation of "you Fiends and Furies (if yet any bee Worse than ourselues)," is within the Medea-Circe tradition.

One of these weird masquers, the Ninth hag, when accounting for her activities, declares:

> And I ha' bene plucking, plants among,
> Hemlock, Henbane, Adders-tongue,
> Night-shade, Moone wort, Lizzards-bane;
> And, twise, by the Doggs was like to be tane.
>
> (187–90)

To make it clear that these particular herbs belong more to the enchantress than to the white magician, Jonson provides scrupulous footnotes about them, stating that Paracelsus, Della Porta, and Agrippa believe these particular poisonous agents to be used in sorcery and not in white magic.[9] Even the stage direction that precedes the Dame's invocation provides a historical survey of the major classical predecessors of the enchantress.[10]

---

8. *The Haddington Masque* of one year earlier had contained an embryonic anti-masque. Ben Jonson, *Works,* ed. by C. H. Herford and Percy and Evelyn Simpson (Oxford, 1941), 7:243–63.

9. "*Cicuta, Hyoscyamus, Ophioglosson, Solanum, Martagon, Doronicu, Aconitum* are the common *veneficall* ingredients; remembered by *Paracelsus, Porta, Agrippa,* and others, which make her to haue gatherd, as a-bout a Castle, Church, or some such vast building (kept by Doggs) among ruines, and wild heapes" (*Ibid.,* p. 293, n. 9).

10. "Here the *Dame* put her selfe into the midst of them, and beganne her following invocation; wherein she tooke occation to boast all the power attributed to witches by the *Antients:* of which euery *Poet* (or the most) doth diue some. Homer to *Circe,* in Odyss. *Theocritus* to *Simantha,* in *Pharmaceutria.* Virgil to *Alphesiboeus,* in his. *Ouid* to *Dipsas* in *Amor.* to *Medea* & *Circe,* in *Metamorph.* Tibullus to *Saga. Horace* to *Canidia, Sagana, Veia, Folio, Seneca* to *Medea,* and the Nurse, in *Herc. Oete. Petr. Arbiter* to his *Saga,* in *Fragment.* And *Claud.* to his *Megoera lib j.* in *Rufinum:* Who takes the habite of a Witch as these doe, and supplies that *historicall* part in the *Poeme,* beside her *morall* person of a Fury. Confirming the same drift, in ours" (*Ibid.,* p. 294). Jonson omits Lucan's Erichtho from this list, though he uses it elsewhere.

As a climax to the antimasque, the witches utter evil charms to evoke chaos and then break into a magical dance. Their efforts are in vain, for their murky living quarters disintegrate, as if through more potent magic. They scatter, revealing the House of Fame, a gorgeous palace, where twelve masquers sit "upon a Throne triumphall, erected in the forme of a *Pyramide,* and circled with all store of light." Fame and the masquers descend in splendor to dance, and in clear possession of the beneficent powers of white magic, celebrate their victory over the witches.

As a device to set up a paradox and strengthen the dualistic opposition that was the essence of the masque, the antimasque was ingenious, for the antimasquers invariably represented misrule, wickedness, or disrespect. Their introduction opened the form up to comic fooling and a measure of satire, both of which are linked to what Jonas Barish terms "a radically theatrical way of dramatizing an antagonism whose essentials can usually be reduced to the terms of a formal dispute."[11] The device reflected the theme of the masque as would a distorting mirror. Even with this new satirical element, however, the brevity of the masque did not permit any extensive or subtle development; restoring the order of the Golden Age still remained its paramount purpose.

Since aristocratic nuptials usually involved courtly celebration, they often provided the occasion for a masque. *The Haddington Masque* (1608)[12] of Jonson, written to follow such a ceremony, avoids the formula of chaos and puts in its place the blessings of Vulcan, who appears as a magician. In creating a spectacular metamorphosis the god commands a rock to cleave,

at which, with a lowd and full musique, the Cliffe parted in the midst, and discouered an illustrious *Concaue,* fill'd with an ample

11. Jonas A. Barish, *Ben Jonson and the Language of Prose Comedy* (Cambridge, 1960), p. 247.
12. Jonson, pp. 243-63.

and glistening light, in which, an artificiall Sphere was made of sluer, eighteene foot in *Diameter,* that turned perpetually; the *Coluri* were heightened with gold; so were the *Arctick* and *Antarctick* circles, the Tropics, the *Aequinoctiall,* the *Meridian,* and *Horizon;* onely the *Zodiake* was of pure gold: in which, the *Masquers,* under the *Characters* of the twelue *Signes,* were plac'd, answering them in number; whose offices, with the whole frame, as it turned, Vvlcan went forward to describe.

(264–74)

In this elaborately fashioned astrological setting, Vulcan announces that he has forged the perfect proportions of a silver sphere in imitation of the heavenly sphere. He correlates the varying aspects of the marriage to the twelve sacred astrological powers of the zodiac. When later the powers descend to dance, the integration of these heavenly, magical deities with the audience has the effect of blessing the nuptials with the benefits of white magic.

On another occasion, in *The Masque of Augures* (1622),[13] Jonson explores augury and divination as a device to congratulate the King handsomely on his role as peacekeeper, or averter of chaos, "whilst the world about him is at odds." Augury was apparently acceptable to this knowledgeable audience as a royal compliment.

As the father of augury who benevolently brings order to the situations, Apollo is described as one

> That can both hurt, and heale; and with his voyce
> Reare Townes, and make societies rejoyce;
> That taught the Muses all their harmonie,
> And men the tunefull Art of Augurie.

(278–81)

He creates a "college of tuneful augurs," who dance themselves into a "prophetic trance," and sing a song whose words explore the art of forecasting events and suggest what birds the augurer should watch for:

---

13. *Ibid.,* pp. 623–47.

Which way, and whence the lightning flew,
Or how it burned, bright, and blew,
Designe, and figure by your lights:
Then forth, and shew the severall flights
Your Birds have made, or what the wing,
Or voyce in Augurie doth bring.
Which hand the Crow cried on, how high
The Vulture, or the Erne did flie,
What wing the Swan made, and the Dove,
The Storke, and which did get above:
Shew all the Birds of food or Prey,
But passe by the unluckie Jay,
The Night-Crow, Swallow or the Kite,
Let those have neither right,
Nor part,
In this nights art.

(346–62)

Naturally Apollo's interpretation of the dance of the
Augurs is auspicious:

The Signes are luckie all, and right,
There hath not beene a voyce, or flight
Of ill Presage.

(368–70)

This is especially so because not only has the dove been
seen, who "brings her augury alone to kings, but Minerva
and her owl have proclaimed the King's control of the
course of events."

This deferential tribute would obviously have pleased
James on Twelfth Night, the occasion of the masque's
performance. Apollo, the mythological god, affirms the
King's role and benevolently applauds the prolonged peace-
ful years of James's reign, conjecturing that his life will
continue to be free from chaos, hatred, and faction. But
Apollo also sounds a warning note in the midst of his
eulogy: the Fates, he says, conceal some truths even from
the gods. The masque concludes reassuringly, however,

with the heavens opening to reveal Jove himself, waiting
with the Senate of the Gods for Apollo's return.

The figure of Orpheus, who also appears frequently in
masques, represents a special tie between the masque and
white magic, since white magicians often use his hymns for
their evocative powers. In Campion's *The Lord's Masque*
(1613), Orpheus asks Mania to set Eutheus (poetic
frenzy) free, it being Jove's wish. Orpheus then sings and
"eight stars of extraordinary bigness" appear. With them
is Prometheus, who persuasively calls on Orpheus to

> apply thy music, for it well
> Helps to induce a courtly miracle.

Here Jonson advocates some poetic frenzy in this world as
a token of chaos both acceptable and appreciated. This
masque also contains other elements of white magic, an
old prophetess, Sibylla, who predicts a happy future for
bride and groom, and the magical effect of bringing silver
statues to life after an invocation,[14] a device similar to one
used by Francis Beaumont in *The Masque of the Inner
Temple* and *Gray's Inn* (1613). The reverse process takes
place in Ben Jonson's *The Golden Age Restored* (1616)
when Pallas confronts the Evils with her shield and turns
them to statues.

One of Jonson's favorite butts for satirical reproof is
white magic, both in *The Alchemist,* one of his most popular
plays, and in a lesser known masque, such as *Mercury Vin-
dicated from the Alchemists at Court* (1616). The gist of
this latter work focuses upon alchemy as well as the Renaissance debate of Art versus Nature.[15] A confrontation develops when one of the Cyclops in Vulcan's alchemical
workshop claims that the fire in the furnace is the "soule
of Art" and that the times prefer Art to Nature. Mercury,

---

14. See Campion, pp. 188-200.
15. See Edward Tayler, *Nature and Art in Renaissance Literature,* New
York, 1964.

in opposition, is convinced that these "smoaky" philosophers commit "treason against Nature." Leaping from the furnace, he enumerates the harassments he had been subjected to by the "sonnes of Art":

> I am their Crude, and their Sublimate; their Praecipitate, and their vnctuous; their male and their female; sometimes their *Hermaphrodite;* what they list to stile me. It is I, that am corroded, and exalted, and sublim'd, and reduc'd, and fetch'd ouer, and filtred, and wash'd, and wip'd; what betweene their salts and their sulphures; their oyles, and their tartars, their brines and their vinegars, you might take me out now a sous'd *Mercury,* now a salted *Mercury,* now a smoak'd and dri'd *Mercury,* now a pouldred and pickl'd *Mercury.*
>
>   (51–60)[16]

In a volatile crescendo he spews out his indictments of them:

> My whole life with 'hem hath been an exercise of torture; one, two, three, foure and fiue times an houre ha' they made mee dance the *Philosophicall* circle, like an Ape through a hoope, or a dogge in a wheele. I am their turne-spit indeed: They eate or smell no rost-meate but in my name. I am their bill of credit still, that passes for their victuals and house-roome. It is through mee, they ha' got this corner o' the Court to coozen in, where they sharke for a hungry diet below staires, and cheat vpon your vnder-Officers, promising mountaines for their meat, and all vpon *Mercuries* security.
>
>   (61–72)

Alchemists sought survival at court, first by promising untold wealth from the philosopher's stone; and then by promising rejuvenation to the aged and virginity to "crack'd maidenheads" through the imbibing of *aurum potabile.*

In the first antimasque, Vulcan and a troupe of "threadbare Alchymists" endeavor to capture the protean Mercury, "whilst he defends himself with his Caducaeus,"[17] and in turn pleads,

---

17. This was a symbol of the philosopher's stone. The rod itself repre-
16. Jonson, 7:408–17.

The *Genius* of the place defend me! You that are both the *Sol* and *Iupiter* of this spheare, *Mercury* inuokes your majesty against the sooty Tribe here; for in your fauor onely, I growe recouer'd and warme.

(106–9)

Once more the court masque centers about the king, equating him symbolically with the mythological gods as well as the sun.

Mercury senses the King's approval of his defense of Nature and condemns the alleged ability of the philosopher's stone to produce *homunculi;* despite this, his invective culminates in the second antimasque, when alchemically made "imperfect creatures, with helmes of lymbeckes" break into an unnatural, graceless dance.

Afterwards Mercury regains his braggadoccio, attacks this Art and extolls Nature:

Art thou not ashamed, *Vulcan,* to offer in defence of thy fire and Art, against the excellence of the Sunne and Nature, creatures more imperfect, then the very flies and insects, that are her trespasses and scapes? Vanish with thy insolence, thou and thy Imposters, and all mention of you melt, before the maiesty of this light, whose *Mercury* henceforth I professe to be, and neuer againe the *Philosophers.* Vanish, I say, that all who haue but their sense, may see and judge the difference between thy ridiculous monsters, and his absolute features.

(185–95)

To celebrate Nature's victory "the whole Scene" changes "to a glorious boure," where Nature sings "How young and fresh am I tonight." She indicates that her creative powers are copious and very far from dead; thus, following the chief pattern in the masque, order is reestablished, Nature is eulogized, and magic and Art satirically exposed as untruthful.

Alchemy is not the only butt of the satire in Jonson's

---

sented the gold of the philosophers, while the two serpents stood for the male and female principles.

masques. In *The Fortunate Isles and Their Union* (1624), his focus shifts to the relationship of votarists to their spirits. Any belief here that the magus and his Neoplatonic spirits could conduct effective magical experiments becomes completely laughable. The masque's major character, Johphiel, "an airy spirit, and (according to the Magi) the intelligence of Jupiter's sphere," encounters a melancholy student and votary, Merefool, who is disappointed at not receiving the spirit promised to him by the brethren of the "Rosy-Cross." Using his power of invisibility, Johphiel eavesdrops on Merefool and mercilessly comments on the discomfort of the student, who to no avail has rigorously followed the necessary rites of summoning spirits.

Merefool complains that dedication, fasting, poverty, and ritual (those mandatory procedures of the white magician) have not helped him in the slightest:

> Haue I both in my lodging, and my diet,
> My cloaths, and euery other solemne charge
> Obseru'd 'hem! made the naked bords my bed!
> A fagot for my pillow! hungred sore!
>
> . . . Yes, and outwatcht,
> Yea, and out-walked any Ghost aliue
> In solitarie circle, worne my bootes,
> Knees, armes, and elbowes out!
>
> (42–45, 53–56)

Sacrifices of the flesh, he confesses, have only brought "a cold wind in my stomach." Johphiel then reveals himself and claims to be an agent of the magician, one Father Outis,[18] Johphiel's fictitious creation. Teasing, fabricating, and generating hope in Merefool, Johphiel claims that he has just come from "this good old hermit,"

> that built
> The Castle in the aire, where all the Brethren

---

18. "Outis" means "no one" in Greek.

Rhodostaurotick liue. It flies with wings,
And runnes on wheeles. . . .

(98–101)[19]

He goads Merefool, playing a trick to convince him that
not only have his vows been heard but that the hermit has
just died in his one hundred and twenty-fifth year, endowing
the student with all his skills and secrets. Wondering where
he may inherit these new offices, Merefool learns that they
are

> In the vpper Region:
> And that you'll find. The Farme of the great Customes,
> Through all the Ports of the Aires Intelligences;
> Then Constable of the Castle *Rosy-Crosse:*
> Which you must be, and Keeper of the Keyes
> Of the whole *Kaball,* with the Seales; you shall be
> Principall Secretarie to the Starres;
> Know all their signatures, and combinations,
> The diuine rods, and consecrated roots.
> Why not? Would you turne trees vp like the wind,
> To shew your strength, march ouer heads of armies,
> Or points of pikes, to shew you lightnesse? force
> All doores of arts, with the petarr, of your wit?
> Reade at one view all books? speake all the languages
> Of Seuerall creatures? master all the learnings
> Were, are, or shall be? or, to shew your wealth,
> Open all treasures, hid by nature, from
> The rocke of Diamond, to the mine of Sea-coale?
> Sir, you shall doe it.

(130–48)

In flattering the unlikely candidate with promises of a magician's powers, Johphiel swiftly touches upon cabala, astrology, staffs, and herbs—all aids of the white magician—and
then proceeds to more Circe-like black magic, such as raising the winds, controlling armies, mastering enormous areas
of knowledge, and finally discerning the secrets of nature

---

19. Rhodostaurotick, or Rosy-Cross, represents the Rosicrucians, magical
sect that Jonson satirizes throughout this masque.

in minerals. Johphiel also praises poverty and humility as necessary attributes of such new learning:

> When you ha' made
> Your glasses, gardens in the depth of winter,
> Where you will walke inuisible to Man-Kind,
> Talkt with all birds & beasts in their own language,
> When you haue penetrated hills like ayre,
> And riss' againe like corke; walk't in the fire
> As 'twere a *Salamander,* past through all
> The winding orbes, like an Intelligence,
> Vp to the *Empyreium,* when you haue made
> The World your gallery, can dispatche a businesse
> In some three minutes, with the *Antipodes,*
> And in fiue more, negotiate the *Globe* ouer;
> You must be poore still.
>
> (167–80)

Johphiel, as an ever-ready spirit, promises Merefool incredible powers:

> I will but touch your temples,
> The corners of your eyes, and tinct the tip,
> The very tip o' your nose, with this *Collyrium,*
> And you shall see i' the aire all the *Ideas,*
> Spirits, and Atomes, Flies, that buz about
> This way, and that way, and are rather admirable,
> Then any way intelligible.
>
> (186–92)

When asked what he would most wish to see, Merefool calls for Zoroaster, "because he's said to be the Father of coniurers, and a cunning man i' the starres." Hermes Trismegistus is suggested as an alternative, as well as Iamblichus, Porphyry, Proclus, Pythagoras, or Plato. Johphiel dismisses Plato's ideas as "now bespoken, at a groat a dozen, three grosse at least," and Pythagoras as having

> rashly run himselfe on an imployment,
> Of keeping *Asses* from a field of beanes;
> And cannot be stau'd off.
>
> (256–58)

Moreover, Plato is unavailable for summoning because

> he is now
> Inventing a rare Mouse-trap with *Owles* wings
> And a *Catts*-foote, to catch the Mise alone:
> And *Aesop,* he is filing a *Fox* tongue,
> For a new fable he has made of Court.
>
> (268–72)

Johphiel promises Merefool that he will see these men, providing he "asks in season," and preferably at Christmas, "when disguising is afoote." Anointing Merefool's eyes and temples, Johphiel turns first to conjuring up Skelton, the early Tudor Poet Laureate to whom was attributed a collection of jests, and then Scogan, the court fool of Edward IV, who was believed to have written another such collection. When they arrive, dressed "in like habits as they lived," Johphiel praises their attributes, asking them which figure he should call up for Merefool's inspection, Hermes or Howleglass, the Till Eulenspiegl hero of a German medieval story. Breaking into Skeltonic rhyme, they call into the antimasque such figures as Elinor Rumming from Skelton's poem, Long Meg of Westminster, Tom Thumb, and Doctor Rat from *Gammer Gurton's Needle.* After their dance, the spirits disappear, much to the regret of Merefool, whom Johphiel now exposes as a gull for believing in the Rosy-Cross. Once Merefool is dismissed, Johphiel changes his tune and the remainder of the masque praises Neptune, who unites the Fortunate Islands, one of which is Britannia "where the happy spirits live."

As a court entertainment, the masque flowered in Jonson's hands, but with Milton's *Comus,* performed in Ludlow Castle in 1634, it moves out of the framework of the court: the audience receives fewer compliments and participates less, and the text is lengthier than that of most masques. Moreover, the victory of reason over libertinism is elevated to a level far beyond that of the masque's more familiar confrontation between order and chaos. Much more mature, this masque presents chaos in terms of the extremely personal crisis of the Lady that is eventually overcome by the white magical figure of the Attendant Spirit.

Comus, the enchanter,[20] son of Circe and Bacchus, "excels his Mother at her mighty Art," by tempting wayfarers with a charmed cup whose potion reduces them to beasts, "to roll with pleasure in a sensual sty." Dwelling in a "leavy Labyrinth," and carrying a charming rod, Comus invokes Cotytto, the "Goddess of Nocturnal sport," performs rites and "dazzling Spells . . . of power to cheat the eye with blear illusion, and give it false presentments," and employs "potent herbs" and "baleful drugs," which "in pleasing slumber lull'd the sense, and in sweet madness robb'd it of itself." He feigns friendliness to the Lady of the masque and takes her to his "Necromancer's hall," holding her captive in an Enchanted Chair.

Comus appeals to what he hopes is her natural sense of lust:

> Wherefore did Nature pour her bounties forth
> With such a full and unwithdrawing hand
> Covering the earth with odors, fruits, and flocks,
> Thronging the Seas with spawn innumerable
> But all to please and sate the curious taste.
>
> (710–14)[21]

His prisoner resists his speech as well as his enchanted cup, and, making "a journey like the path to Heaven," embraces

---

20. The enchanter theme becomes mechanical and hollow by the time of Aurelian Townshend's *Tempe Restored* (1632)—another masque of Circe and her prisoners—and William Davenant's *The Temple of Love* (1634), which explores the court's fascination for Platonic love:

> New Sects of Love;
> Which must not woo or court the person, but
> The mind; and practice generation not of bodies
> but of souls.

See William Davenant, *Works* (London, 1872) 1:287–305.

21. John Milton, *Complete Poems and Major Prose*, ed. Merritt Y. Hughes (New York, 1957).

both Christian tradition and Platonic faith, for her virtue requires the protection of Christian grace. Her rejection of appetite is her victory in a trial of Christian virtue, even though she remains imprisoned in the Enchanted Chair.[22] Her two brothers, unable to rescue the Lady through mere force, enlist the aid of the Attendant Spirit, a daemon who gives them some haemony, "a small unsightly root," whose "leaf was darkish,"[23] and tells them it

> more med'cinal is than the Moly
> That Hermes once to wise Ulysses gave;
> He call'd it Haemony, and gave it me,
> And Bade me keep it as of sovran use
> 'Gainst all enchantments, mildew blast, or damp
> Or ghastly furies' apparition.
>
> (636–41)

Its superlative magical property protects them in their assault on Comus's lair, where they break his enchanted cup, but fail to snatch his wand.[24] The Spirit then calls upon the nymph Sabrina, a martyred virgin, who claims " 'tis my office best to help ensnared chastity," and she releases the Lady from the Enchanted Chair by performing a white magical task with "drops that from my fountain pure I have kept of precious cure" (912-13). A joyous climax is ensured when the Attendant Spirit presents the Lady and her two brothers to their parents. As these masquers happen to be the children of the Earl of Bridgewater, who commissioned the work, Milton, the Christian humanist, does

---

22. See William G. Madsen, "The Idea of Nature in Milton's Poetry," in *Three Studies in the Renaissance* (New Haven, 1958), pp. 198-215, for a discussion of grace, nature, chastity, and virginity.

23. See Milton, p. 105, n. 636, for further information on moly and aemony. The Trinity College, Cambridge, manuscript of *Comus* lists the Attendant Spirit as a daemon, the kind of spirit that a white magician utilizes.

24. See John G. Demaray, *Comus as a Masque* (New York, 1969), pp. 249-50. Demaray states that wands, potions, and herbs do have allegorical meanings, but he believes that the cup and the potion are the only magical objects in *Comus*. Moreover, he does not concede that there is much Neo-platonic influence in the masque.

homage both to their father on earth and to their heavenly Father.

The beneficent Attendant Spirit, who is from Jove's court, is a spirit such as the white magician might try to attract to the sublunary world.[25] His "safe convoy" is toward the heavenly "crown that Virtue gives" and he is able to disguise his appearance and play his pipe with the same magical effect that Orpheus achieves with his soft Pipe and smooth-dittied Song (86). The effect is the very reverse of the enchanter's ability to stir up chaos, for the Spirit brings temperance, celestial harmony, and divine order to nature. As in so many masques, the battle against chaos is won and a daemonic spirit, such as might aid a white magician, nullifies the unruly enchanter's magic.

As a highly specialized form of coterie entertainment, the masque as well as more public forms of theater could not survive the chaos of the Civil War. The king, as an all-beneficent symbol of divine and white magical powers who was capable of creating order from chaos, became a bankrupt fantasy. The milieu for displaying such figures of wish-fulfillment no longer existed, and the nostalgia of tranquilizing platitudes had no place in the Interregnum.

---

25. Evidently, the Attendant Spirit has more mobility than Prospero's Ariel, for he can fly to the moon and presumably above it to Jove's court:

> "I can fly, or I can run
> Quickly to the green earth's end
> Where the bow'd welkin slow doth bend,
> And from thence can soar as soon
> To the corners of the Moon."
> (113–17)

7

Antecedents of *The Alchemist*

*T*he revival of satire in the English Renaissance owed
its existence to the climate of the times, and to a tradition that was primarily dependent upon a Juvenalian flaying
of vice, though it also drew, in part, upon Aristophanic Old
Comedy. Juvenal had unleashed both spite and indignation
upon a corrupt society, his villains becoming targets of scorn
through their treacherous words and deeds. A Stoic moral-
ist with a majestic style, he wrote in condemnation of many
contemporaries. Aristophanes, however, had written un-
sentimental comedy, whose figures existed in a world of
incongruous extremes, a world constructed for the purpose
of making an intellectual joke about such subjects as politics,
citizenship, or education.[1] Indebted more to Juvenal, Ben

---

1. Aristophanes spoke didactically through the *parabasis*, when the Chorus
addressed the audience, and the chorus-leader made satirical comments
upon contemporary issues in Athenian society. The *parabasis* dropped any
aura of dramatic illusion, and the chorus spoke unsentimentally and directly
for the author. In addition, they could divide into two sections which de-
bated the pros and cons of an issue. The winner, of course, posed the viewpoint of the author.
 Caricature was a means of achieving satiric effect. Demagogues, for
example, were caricatured in *The Knights,* the Sophists in *The Clouds,*
and the judicial system in *The Wasps.*

Jonson, a railer and a malcontent commentator, had an unerring eye for human weaknesses and deftly set them up as targets for his critical shots. The weaknesses he most frequently attacked were greed and lust, qualities that in an earlier age had received theatrical treatment as morality-play vices. Alchemy became especially synonymous with greed for Jonson, who, as the preceding chapter indicates, made an acute and detailed examination of white magic. Although many had believed in alchemy from early to medieval times, more tended toward disbelief by the seventeenth century, making it particularly ripe for satire. By creating in his play *The Alchemist* (1610) a charlatan magician who was the antithesis of everything that the consecrated white magician symbolized, Jonson turned white magic into a further target for reproof, most definitely nothing to be held in awe. Last in a long line of celebrated writers who successfully satirized alchemy, Jonson was the most effective. To illuminate the subtleties of his play, it is helpful to ascertain public views of charlatan alchemists as well as those literary traditions of satirizing white magic and alchemy on which Jonson drew.

As those eager for gain are often the easiest to gull, it is no surprise that alchemy was the field of white magic that most appealed to charlatans. Greed enticed the rich sponsor who desired greater wealth, and greed drove the charlatan who desired both survival and wealth, especially if he could enjoy both in the comfortable quarters of his gullible patron.

But, of course, there was also skepticism about alchemy. For instance, Vincent of Beauvais included in his vast compendium of learning, the *Speculum majus* (1485), a segment devoted to nature and chemistry, called *Speculum naturale*. In it, Vincent proclaims the impossibility of transmutation, but concedes that it is possible to change white metal,

to a yellow color so that it may seem to be gold, also by removing the impurities of lead so that it may seem to be silver; but it will always be really lead: but they produce in it such qualities that they may deceive men in it. For the rest, I do not believe it possible that a specific difference in any innate quality can be removed. But there is effected a removal (or change, "expoliatio") of its accidental qualities as color, flavor or weight. The works of art also are not of the same kind as the works of nature, nor so certain although they may be kindred and similar. For art is more feeble than nature, nor can it overtake it without great labor.[2]

(8: 90)

Vincent's thinking was, nevertheless, ambivalent: after first expressing doubt about the efficacy of alchemy, he then states that,

it may be seen that alchemy may be to a certain degree false (or fraudulent, "falsa") nevertheless it is true that by the ancient philosophers and by artizans in our time it has been proven to be true.

(8:85)[3]

Albertus Magnus also doubted. He believed alchemists to be fabricators of a metal that superficially resembled gold, and stated that he knew of no alchemist

but that he rather colors with a yellow elixir into an appearance of gold, and with a white elixir colors to the resemblance of silver, seeking that the color may remain while in the fire and may penetrate the whole metal, just as a spirit (spiritualis substantia) is introduced into medicines, and in this manner of working it is possible to produce a yellow color, the substance of the metal remaining. And here again it is not to be maintained that several kinds of metal are contained in one another. It is from this and similar things that is demolished the dictum of those who say that any kind of metal you please is contained in another.[4]

A further thirteenth-century philosopher, Roger Bacon,

---

2. Vincent of Beauvais, *Speculum naturale* (Nuremberg, 1485), 2 vols., quoted by John Maxon Stillman in *The Story of Alchemy* (New York, 1960), p. 170.

3. Beauvais, p. 170.

4. Albertus Magnus, *Mineralium,* III, Tract I, chap. 8, quoted in Stillman, p. 252.

gave far more credence to the potentials of alchemy, "which teaches how to make the noble metals, and colors and many other things better or more abundantly by art (artificium) than they are made in nature."[5] He also believed in the life-prolonging potentials of the products of alchemy. Yet he concurred that there were remarkably few men who comprehended either how to make colors and metals or how to compose medicines for the lengthening of life. The alchemist's elixir removed all impurities from baser metals so that it became the purest silver or gold. When imbibed, it was also believed to remove all impurities from the body and restore it to a new life. Bacon claimed these manifold processes to be purification, distillation, ablution, grinding, roasting, calcination, mortification, sublimation, proportion, incineration, decomposition, solidification, fixation, cleansing, liquefaction, and projection.

From the first to the last of these procedures, there obviously were many potential pitfalls. The genuine white magician might well founder and attain neither gold nor silver. The charlatan, however, could employ this series of convoluted experiments to delay the unveiling of any tangible product. An infinite variety of disasters could be manufactured so that work might begin all over again. However he accomplished it, the major task of the masquerading charlatan was to arouse new hopes of success.

The lure of gold undoubtedly enticed men of means and heads of state to support the charlatan in his guise of dedicated white magician. Greed dimmed the skepticism of guarantors. For a while, each saw the activities of his private alchemist as unimpeachable. Yet, at some point, the charlatan was almost sure to be unmasked, his experiment then immediately proven a worthless fabrication. Once more he was on the run, eventually, though at a distance, to perpetrate a similar fraud on yet another gullible sponsor.[6]

5. *Ibid.,* p. 261.
6. Leonhard Thurneysser, who was born in Basel in 1530, led a checkered

Skeptical disbelief in white magic appears in fictional nondramatic form in Lucian and far earlier; it is equally strong in Chaucer; and it reappears *a fortiori* in Erasmus's *Colloquies*. A look at the place of charlatans in the plots of these works provides a unique and necessary prelude to an examination of Jonson's play.[7]

Lucian inherited the mantle of Aristophanes, composing satires that probed the absurdities of fraud and superstition and, in particular, lambasted magic and necromancy. At this time, during the second century of Christianity, when hedonism and superstition pervaded the Roman Empire, anyone sufficiently unscrupulous could set himself up as a practicing magician—whether astrologer or oracular prophet—and conduct a thriving business enterprise by exploiting the needs of a gullible and superstitious people. Lucian bore down upon such practices, not caustically attacking his victims as did Juvenal or Swift, but constructing a hard core of reality as an alternative to fraudulent activity.

Based upon the story of a man who succeeds in fabricating a new god and establishing an oracle, *Alexander the Quack Prophet* admirably demonstrates Lucian's indignant attitude toward charlatanism. Alexander gains both suppliants and profits by successfully executing a series of ruthless tricks, for

in brains and shrewdness and keenness there wasn't anybody like him. Energy, grasp, memory, a natural aptitude for learning— he had more than his due of each. But he used these endowments for the worst possible ends. Though he had such a wealth of noble talents, he lived in a way that outdid all the notorious evildoers of history. . . . You must conjure up in your mind a soul

career of duplicity. He gained the support of the Archduke Ferdinand of Austria, who sent him on travels throughout Europe for the purpose of alchemical research. The charlatan's operations were exposed as swindles in several German cities, and he was obliged to flee. One of his devices was, on arrival in a new city, to stage an elaborate display of accumulated wealth and claim that alchemy was the cause of it. See Stillman, p. 355.

7. Jonson is believed to have read these and other works before writing *The Alchemist* (Jonson, 10:147).

composed of the most varied ingredients, one that blended deceit, trickery, lying, sharp practices, carelessness, nerve, recklessness, and tirelessness in conjuring out plans with trust, reliability, and the knack of acting a better role, of looking white when the end in view was black.[8]

Although the chameleon-like Alexander feigns honorableness, as a youth one of his friends was a quack who taught him "magic, miracle-working incantations, charms to snare a lover, tricks to defeat an enemy, places to dig for buried treasure, and ways to inherit a fortune."[9] Succeeding to this catalogue of tricks at the quack's death, Alexander enters another association in which both partners are "masquerading as magicians, pulling off swindles, and fleecing the 'fatheads.' "[10]

Alexander employs the premise that most men are at the mercy of hope and fear and will pay freely for knowledge of the future. With the expertise of a showman, he stages several spectacular events to introduce his oracle and convince his audience that the oracle is connected with both Apollo and Asclepius, so that "the mob followed him en masse, everyone in a frenzy and crazed with expectations."[11] Inside a dim cell, he flaunts a huge serpent that in only a few days has supposedly attained this size through the aid of magic. Nobody senses a hoax. Rather, the throngs are convinced it is a miracle and that a god exists within the oracle.

Meanwhile, with the aid of an ever-growing staff, Alexander reads all written requests to the oracle, reseals them, and returns them to the suppliants, resourcefully providing each with a tantalizing, enigmatic answer. His agents visit adjacent lands to advertise his skill in everything from prophecy to necromancy. "A good many men of sense"

8. Lucian, *Selected Satires,* trans. and ed. Lionel Casson (New York, 1962), p. 270.
9. *Ibid.,* p. 271.
10. *Ibid.,* pp. 271-72.
11. *Ibid.,* p. 276.

finally unmask the questionable performances. But the charlatan retaliates with slander, and such is the tremendous
popularity of the oracle that his business still burgeons. Since
all supplications to the oracle fall into his hands, he black-
mails the more indiscreet petitioners, hires agents to report
to him the needs of his clients, blasphemes against Epicureans,
whom he considers exposers and enemies, and finds time to
sleep with the wives of the men he has duped.

The author himself steps into his own story at this point
to denounce Alexander and become the charlatan's worst
enemy. Alexander responds by trying to have Lucian
drowned at sea, but the venture is unsuccessful. Eventually
old age and a diseased body bring about the false prophet's
death. By that time Lucian has built a detailed indictment
of the superstitions that debase men and make them victims
of their own fears, while brilliantly satirizing charlatanism
and condemning those who prey on gullibility.

Writing very much later than Lucian, Chaucer exposes
charlatanism in alchemical practices in "The Canon's Yeoman's Tale." Like Jonson, Chaucer expresses both belief
and disbelief in white magic. He gently satirizes his Doctour
of Physik, who, being "grounded in astronomye . . . kepte
his pacient a ful greet deel in houres by his magyk natureel."
His remedies are governed by the currently accepted
notions of astrological readings, as well as by a knowledge
of the four humors.

> Wel koude he fortunen the ascendent
> Of his ymages for the pacient.
> He knew the cause of everich maladye,
> Were it of hoot, or coold, or moyst, or drye,
> And where they engendered, and of what humour.
>   (417–21)[12]

In an earlier work, Chaucer has already displayed a knowledge of magic, including within *The House of Fame* a

---

12. Geoffrey Chaucer, "General Prologue" to the *Canterbury Tales*, in *Works*, 2nd ed., ed. F. N. Robinson (Cambridge, Mass., 1957).

gathering of every conceivable kind of dealer in magic, both black and white. His white magicians, the "clerkes," employ natural magic and astrology in their cures and, like the Doctour of Physik, construct images of their patients to induce magical aid.[13]

Chaucer's doctor appears convinced of the value of astrology in cures; his Yeoman's views on alchemy, however, are filled with foreboding. When urged on by the Host, the Yeoman reveals so true a picture of the fickle and frustrating nature of alchemy, that his master, the Canon, who conducts such experiments, leaves the pilgrims and rides away in high dudgeon. The Yeoman then exposes the physical hazards of the Canon's pursuit:

> I am so used in the fyr to blowe
> That it hath chaunged my colour, I trowe,
> I am nat wont in no mirour to prie,
> But synke soore and lerne multiplie.
> We blondren evere and pouren in the fir,
> And for al that we faille in oure desir,
> For evere we lakken oure conclusioun.
> To muchel folk we doon illusioun,
> And borwe gold, be it a pound or two,
> Or ten, or twelve, of manye sommes mo,
> And make hem wenen, at the leeste weye,
> That of a pound we kowde make tweye.
>   (666–77)

---

13.   Ther saugh I pleye jugelours,
             Magiciens, and tregetours,
             And Phitonesses, charmeresses,
             Olde wicches, sorceresses,
             That use exorsisacions,
             And eke these fumygacions;
             And clerkes eke, which konne wel
             Al this magik naturel,
             That craftely doon her ententes
             To make, in certeyn ascendentes,
             Ymages, lo, thrugh which magik
             To make a man ben hool or syk.
                              (1259–70)
Chaucer also mentions that he saw Circe, Medea, Calypso, Hermes Ballenus (a follower of Trismegistus), and Simon Magus in *The House of Fame*.

He believes the attempt to raise base metals into gold to be a foolish myth, one that usually leaves the practitioner in beggary rather than riches:

> Yet is it fals, but ay we han good hope
> It for to doon, and after it we grope,
> But that science is so fer us biforn,
> We mowen nat, although we hadden sworn,
> It overtake, it slit awey so faste.
> It sole us maken beggers atte laste.
>
> (678–83)

In the style of a complaint, the Yeoman depicts his grim seven-year existence at "that slidynge science" with the Canon. From this he emerges with nothing but debts accumulated by borrowing gold in order to make more gold. Yet he also outlines his considerable skill and knowledge of the alchemical craft, informing the pilgrims of the four spirits—quicksilver, arsenic, sulphur, and sal ammoniac—as well as of the correspondences between the planets and metals. He gives short shrift to both the philosopher's stone and the elixir of life, and adds that there are many accidents and explosions that lead to litigious discussions over whether correct proportions and procedures were observed in the experiment:

> We faille of that which that we wolden have,
> And in our madnesse everemore we rave.
> And whan we been togidres everichoon,
> Every man semeth a Salomon.
> But al thyng which shineth as the gold
> Nis nat gold, as that I have herd it told;
> Ne every appul that is faire at eye
> Ne is not good, what so men clappe or crye.
> Right so, lo, fareth it amonges us:
> He that semeth the wiseste, by Jhesus!
> Is moost fool, whan it cometh to the preef;
> And he that semeth trewest is a theef.
>
> (958–69)

The Yeoman's embittered autobiographical sketch serves as a warning to would-be dabblers in alchemy. It is a shrewd and telling commentary on a profession that some of Chaucer's readers must have suspected to be fraudulent. This effective plaint, moreover, acts as a prelude to the more satirical story, in which the Canon is characterized: "in al this world of falshede nis his peer." The falseness of the charlatan's sleight-of-hand tricks and the blissful unawareness of the duped priest then becomes the tale's coexisting themes.

At the start of the story, the Yeoman's master, the Canon, gains the confidence of a susceptible, innocent priest and asks him to provide three ounces of mercury and a fire of coals. To the accompaniment of much Christian philosophy, he promises an alchemical conversion of the mercury into silver. Continuing his strategy, the trickster demands privacy "whils that we werke in this philosophie." Later, he places a crosslet filled with a spectacularly burning powder in the fire to produce a dazzling blaze. Then, while the attention of the priest is diverted, the Canon slips silver into the crosslet and "glad in every veyne was the priest, when he saugh that it was so."

In a second experiment, the priest is duped once more, and yet a third time. At this point, the Canon, "Who semed freendly to hem that knewe him not," calls for copper in the crosslet and by further sleight of hand substitutes a silver for a copper plate. The gullible priest is utterly delighted, and asks the price of the recipe. The Canon, in turn, claims that in all of England only two people know the secret: himself and a friar. Forty pounds is the selling price: the Canon pockets this money, demands secrecy, and then disappears.

The Yeoman reminds the reader "how that, in ech estaat, betwixe men and gold ther is debaat. . . ." He maintains, however, that so many are involved in hazarding initial amounts of gold for the attempted "multiplying" of

alchemy, that gold has become scarce. He jests at the
mystery and secrecy with which such philosophers surround
their rites; scorning the promised gains of alchemy, he
warns all to flee these operations:

> O! fy, for shame, they that han been brent,
> Allas! kan nat flee the fires heete?
> Ye that it use, I rede ye it leete,
> Lest ye lese al; for bet than nevere is late.
>
> (1407–10)

Finally, he reports that Plato, when questioned about
how to make the philosopher's stone, took the secretive
position usual to all magicians, using Christ as his authority:

> "Nay, nay," quod Plato, "certein, that I nyl.
> The philosophres sworn were everychon
> That they sholden discovere it unto noon,
> Ne in no book it write in no manere.
> For unto Christ it is so lief and deere
> The he wol nat that it discovered bee,
> But where is liketh to his deitee
> Men fer t'enspire, and eele for to deffende
> Whom that hymn liketh; lo, this is the ende."
>
> (1463–71)

Far less complaint and more mirth characterize the
satire on alchemy ("a notorious disease") that Erasmus
published in his *Colloquies* in 1524.[14] Like Chaucer, Erasmus
takes an anticlerical point of view. In this case, however, the
priest is the guller, and the dupe a man named Balbinus,
who is immersed in "sacred studies." Bandying about before
Balbinus such fabricated terms as "longation" and "curta-
tion," the priest removes suspicion of fraud, finds he has a
sponsor, and plants his year-long "experiment" in Balbinus's
house. At each turn, whatever gold the rich man offers

---

14. Erasmus, *Ten Colloquies,* trans. Craig R. Thompson (New York,
1957), p. 53. See also, in the same edition, "Exorcism," pp. 37–46, in which
Erasmus provides a witty criticism of duping through the feigned use of
spirits.

toward the project, whether it be for starting the furnace, supplying wood for fuel, buying fresh glasses, or making offerings to the Virgin Mary, is put by the priest into whoring, gaming, and drinking. Using whatever procrastinatory devices he can devise, he extracts as much from his sponsor as possible, and when nothing is forthcoming in the experiments, claims that Balbinus is not sufficiently devout. Later, the priest asserts that their experiments have become common knowledge and their alchemical activities will be regarded as a capital offense. The priest, "a master of rhetoric," hammering away at every position, suggests the likelihood of the death penalty for their crime. Balbinus, eager to prevent arrest, yields to the priest's blackmail and gives him an enormous sum. The priest, of course, pockets the money and begins once more to stoke the furnace, while the gullible Balbinus lives on in eternal hope.

Finally, when the priest is caught trespassing in the bedroom of a courtier's wife, he is told by his sponsor that sin blocks a successful outcome to alchemy. Yet, again the priest is ready with a trick. He claims that the Virgin Mary miraculously aided his safe escape from the escapade. Balbinus, gullible as always, is so touched that he forgives all. Not until the priest's actual feigning is revealed by a friend does Balbinus shamefacedly provide the charlatan with travel money. He orders him to leave and asks him not to share with anyone the details of his duplicity:

> The imposter was in no danger. He understood the "art" about as well as an ass does, and in an affair of this kind swindling is regarded leniently. Besides, if he had attempted robbery, benefit of clergy would have saved him from hanging. Nor would anyone willingly be at the expense of keeping him in jail.[15]

Throughout its existence, white magic is suspect and vulnerable to satire. Lucian, Chaucer, and Erasmus all make it clear that it is an open door for any charlatan to enter. A

---

15. *Ibid.,* p. 55.

rogue's skilled powers of suggestion and persuasiveness are at their best when used in a pursuit about which an unsuspecting client knows little but believes much. By exploiting this belief the trickster can pose as the white magician of popular imagination without needing to be deeply conversant with the actual procedures of an initiate.

As actual philosophers of white magic in the Renaissance, it is significant here that both Bruno and Della Porta wrote plays to express their own satirical indictments of the charlatan practice, works that are not only representative of a continuing tradition but that also form a significant bridge between earlier nondramatic satire of white magic and Jonson's satire for the stage. In *Candelaio,* a play that exposes a "cheating alchemist" as well as a charlatan magician, Bruno focuses his satirical commentary on the foibles of an articulate group of Neapolitans.[16] Particularly of interest here are Cencio, the "cheating alchemist . . . the most detestable of all nature's work," and Scaramuré, the charlatan magician. Both are conceived as parasites on society, and even though their roles are not large, their presence supports two of the play's three major themes.

Bruno's play provides a witty insight into the practices of those charlatans with whom he, as a philosopher of magic, may have wished to dissociate himself. On a more general level, his satire of alchemy is part of the tradition that influenced Jonson: both writers emphasize the duping of willing fools rather than the seriousness of alchemy itself; both share the assumption that their audiences are conversant with some of the traditional knowledge of magic; and both make use of the skeptic to expose false practitioners.

Della Porta, a contemporary of Bruno and a man of eclectic interests, was led to white magic through such divergent pursuits as botany and play-writing. Specialists have conceded, in fact, that in his experiments with the

---

16. Giordano Bruno, *The Candle Bearer* (1582), trans. J. R. Hale, in Eric Bentley, ed., *The Genius of the Italian Theater* (New York, 1964).

nurturing and grafting of plants he made a real contribution to science. In the theater, where he could use his scientific knowledge to indulge his love of wonder-working, his efforts were also well received. One of Della Porta's most successful plays, *Lo Astrologo,* was first performed for King James at Trinity College, Cambridge, in the spring of 1614.[17] As a satire on judicial astrology (the prognostication of events through planetary influences), the play has as its principal figure the charlatan-astrologer Albumazar, a character to whom Subtle in Jonson's *The Alchemist* bears some resemblance. Hugh Dick points out, however, that Jonson's work was written prior to Tomkis's adaptation, although he does not comment on whether or not Jonson may have read the original.

The plot springs from a familiar *commeddia erudita* situation, an old man (Pandolfo), wishing to gain the hand of a young girl (Flavia). Because Pandolfo cannot get the necessary consent of Flavia's father (Antonio), who is presumed lost at sea, he arranges for the services of the "most divine Albumazar," an astrologer who happens to be a charlatan with three thieves as accomplices. To create a substitute for Antonio who will consent to Pandolfo's marriage, Albumazar, using pseudo-magic, attempts to place Antonio's spirit in the body of Trincalo, Pandolfo's farmer. With this scheme the play's preposterous complications begin, unraveling finally as Pandolfo discovers that he has been gulled, the charlatan is undone, and the young lovers are united.

Like earlier plots, *Albumazar* follows traditional comic patterns, presumably appealing to audiences that by the

17. Thomas Tomkis, *Albumazar,* ed. Hugh Dick, *University of California Publications in English* 13 (Los Angeles, 1944). Della Porta's plays were popular for adaptation into English, and especially for the academic stage. For example, *Ignoramus* of George Ruggle is based after *La Trappolara* (Bergamo, 1596); *Labyrinthus* comes from *La Fantesca* (1567), adapted by Walter Hawkesworth. See Mary A. Scott, *Elizabethan Translations after the Italina,* Vassar Semi-Centennial Series (Boston, 1916), pp. 208–9, 211, and 218, quoted by Hugh A. Dick, p. 54.

early seventeenth century had largely grown skeptical of the effectiveness of white magic. More involved with the burgeoning and the new mercantilism of London life, this audience must have found especially humorous the charlatan's feigning of the white magician's religious dedication to his task in order to disguise his single-minded, lucrative gulling of the susceptible and unaware. What better way to discard a former generation's belief in the possibility of white magic than to satirize its trappings in the hands of a trickster? Clearly, as a pivotal comic character, the charlatan white magician, be he astrologist or alchemist, engendered a rapid series of continuing actions based upon guileful manipulations that only foundered when reality dawned on the gullible seekers, revealing his bluff as a tissue of fabrications.

8

Jonson: Alchemy Satirized

*M*ore extensively than any other playwright of the
English Renaissance, Johnson explored the tenets
of white magic and the magicians who held them. His knowledge of practice and malpractice was vast. His charlatans,
active and willful, greedy and lustful, were men of enormous
pretences, well versed in gulling susceptible fools. With
such figures, Jonson maintained and surpassed the tradition
of the charlatan-white magician as he appeared in Lucian,
Chaucer, and Erasmus. Heir to these distinguished predecessors, Jonson also responded to the timeliness of satire in
his own age. Its attempted suppression revealed the vigor
of satire's existence: Jonson's contemporaries, Hall, Guil-
pin, Donne, and Marston, whipped and scourged human
follies, and in the process even embarked upon private
retaliatory skirmishes among themselves, sharpening their
satirical weapons at one another's expense. These personal
attacks scarcely conformed to satire's major aim of explor-
ing generalized qualities,[1] for satire was not a "matter of

1. See John Peter, *Complaint and Satire* (Oxford, 1956).

123

personal resentment, but of impersonal condemnation."[2] Yet, in part, they did serve to create an audience for satire. In his masterful play *The Alchemist*, Jonson's major satirical thrust was the gullibility of greedy, lustful human beings in the hands of cheaters and cozeners. However, he also attacked the spurious white magical means charlatans employed. To draw attention to the manner in which the trio of charlatans involve certain of their clients in false white magical practices is the purpose of this exploration.

The fraud of charlatans, the failure of white magic to find the philosopher's stone, to produce gold, and to discover the elixir of life, had bred skepticism in some by the seventeenth century. Jonson's own skepticism played upon his audiences, both popular and courtly, testing their ambivalence, probing beliefs and disbeliefs in white magic. For example, one of his audience, James I, followed the conventional line of dismissing magic as blasphemous; yet, the reader of his *Daemonologie* cannot fail to detect the King's intense fascination with magic and all its trappings. This notable ambivalence toward white magic was clearly manifested in the almost simultaneous appearance of *The Alchemist* and *The Tempest*. In one, the white magician, as charlatan, was used as an admirable tool for social satire; in the other, he was made genuine, and seen as a symbolic, mythic figure with some of the powers of the *deus ex machina* or the king figure in certain court masques.[3]

As a white magician, the charlatan has the same effect as the disruptive enchanter, or the Vice figure of medieval drama. He confuses and entraps his victims in a chaotic plot of his own making. He manipulates the unsuspecting through their fears and lusts, making false promises to answer their

---

2. Middleton Murry, *The Problem of Style* (London, 1939), p. 56.
3. See Northrop Frye, *A Natural Perspective*, pp. 70-71. "What Shakespeare has that Jonson neither has nor wants is the sense of nature as comprising not merely an order but a power, at once supernatural and connatural, expressed most eloquently in the dance and controlled either by benevolent human magic or by divine will."

immediate needs. In the end, the duped victims pay for their shadowy privileges and the charlatan pockets his gains, his entire behavior being the antithesis of how a consecrated white magician would act. Moreover, the charlatan had a simple, self-protecting device, a defense that could conceal a vast ignorance and leave would-be clients no objective foundation for their hopes. As the true alchemist claimed that only initiates were to be entrusted with the secrets of practice, so charlatans had a perfect excuse to silence enquiries. Indeed, there was for clients little recourse to proof from books: those available included processes but rarely recipes, truths being obscured by archaic symbolism designed only for initiates to comprehend.

Such sleight-of-hand activity is the bluffing of the charlatans in *The Alchemist* that there is nothing but confusion for their credulous clients, who are lured to a London house vacated by its master, Lovewit, on account of the plague. One of the impostors, Jeremy the butler, has invited two disreputable confederates there to set up an alchemical laboratory and divide any of their extorted profits. Jeremy (alias Face), Subtle, and Dol cooperate shakily from the outset, an undercurrent of dissension constantly threatening their mutual confidence until their enterprise finally disintegrates. An initial harangue characterizes their relationship, Face reproaching Subtle for forgetting how Face saved him from starvation,

> when all your *alchemy,* and your *algebra,*
> Your *mineralls, vegetalls,* and *animalls*
> Your coniuring, cosning, and your dosen of trades,
> Could not reliue your corps, with so much linnen
> Would make you tinder, but to see a fire;
> I ga' you count'nance, credit for your coales,
> Your stills, your glasses, your *materialls,*
> Built you a fornance, drew your customers
> Aduanc'd all your black arts; lent you, beside,
> A house to practise in—
>
> (I, i, 38–47)

Insulted by this accusation of "black arts," Subtle counters by asking Face whether he has not been raised by Subtle from squalor:

> *Sublim'd* thee, and *exalted* thee, and *fix'd* thee
> I' the *third region,* call'd our state of grace?
> Wrought thee to spirit, to *quintessence,* with paines
> Would twise haue won me the philosophers worke?
> . . . .
> Made thee a second, in mine owne great art?
> And haue I this for thanks? Doe you rebell?
> Do you file out, i' the proiection?
>
> (I, i, 68–71, 77–79)

This mutual tirade is freely interlaced with terms from white magic, as, for example, the references to the fundamental areas of practice in the beginning of Face's speech and the use of alchemical terms in Subtle's response. Jonson, moreover, italicizes major alchemical expressions throughout his text.[4]

In a final thrust at Subtle, Face, classifying alchemy as in the realm of black magic, thereby produces the worst threat of all, the law:

> I'll bring thee, rogue, within
> The *statute of sorcerie, tricesimo tertio,*
> Of HARRY the eight: I, and (perhaps) thy necke
> Within a nooze, for laundring gold, and barbing it.
>
> (I, i, 111–14)

Interrupting their exchange, Dol reminds them of "the venter *tripartite"* and threatens to resign.

An unsteady truce ensues as a result, Subtle arguing that their separate tasks in the organization make unequal shares, his knowledge of white magic being much the weightier contribution. Not to be outdone, Face rejoins that they would have no customers without his special skill of unearthing them:

---

4. See Paracelsus, *Selected Writings,* ed. Jolande Jacobi (New York, 1951), for a useful glossary of alchemical terms.

Why, now, you smoky persecuter of nature!
Now, doe you see, that some-thing's to be done,
Beside your beech-coale, and your sor'siue waters,
Your crosse-lets, crucibles, and cucurbites?
You must haue stuffe, brought home to you, to worke on?
And, yet, you thinke, I am at no expence,
In searching out these veines, then following 'hem,
Then trying 'hem out. 'Fore god, my intelligence
Costs me more money, than my share oft comes too,
In these rare workes.

(I, iii, 100–109)

Such altercations between the charlatans frequently erupt
during their hasty shifts from one fabricated situation to
the next. When Face eventually breaks the rules of their
tenuous agreement in attempting to gain the hand of Dame
Pliant—one of their clients, a young and well-to-do widow—
this is enough of a betrayal for Subtle to plot to abscond
with both Dol and their total gains. Yet his conniving comes
to naught: at the unexpected arrival of Lovewit, Face
claims that his master has forgiven him and that officers of
the law are about to invade the house. At this ploy, the
devious partnership collapses, Dol and Subtle being thank-
ful enough to flee, penniless.

Prior to this climactic moment, each charlatan has assumed multiple roles, as many and changing as the phases
of alchemical transmutation itself. Readily adapting to the
impulsive requests of hopeful clients, the three in quick
succession feign knowledge of spirits, prophecy, astrology,
fairies, divination, physiognomy, chiromancy, and alchemy,
with its offshoots of the elixir and the philosopher's stone—
all of which have their roots in white magic.

Though Jonson's research of alchemy displays his expertise in and intellectual grasp of all subjects, he places this
lore in the mouths of the charlatans, combining it with their
underground thieves' jargon to render it absurd.[5] Alone,

---

5. Edgar Hill Duncan, "Jonson's *Alchemist* and the Literature of Alchemy," *PMLA* 61 (September 1946):697–710.

the charlatans outrageously abuse or flatter one another; in the company of clients, they act out their charade, mellifluously pronouncing half-understood mystic knowledge with the assumed air of professionals. Bolstering their clients' faltering egos with flattery, the thieves beguile and convince with their euphemisms. Their style is mock heroic and counterfeit, a continual abuse to all decorum.

Duped by Subtle, Dol, and Face, the unwitting clients all undergo undignified initiations into the sphere of false magic. Dapper, the first, a lawyer's clerk, desires to have a familiar spirit to guide him to successful winnings in gambling and horse racing, and, no doubt, a contemporary audience could associate familiar spirits with John Dee, Simon Forman, and Simon Reed, all mystical practitioners of unsavory repute. Both Face and Subtle cleverly play upon the current danger that such men encountered with the law in their use of familiars. Subtle and Face's devious interchange implies terror and needful secrecy, so that the greater Subtle's risk with the law appears to be, the greater the extortion from the eager Dapper, whose familiar is to predict the outcome of all games, and, as Subtle promises, "draw you all the treasures of the realme" with "such vigorous luck as cannot be resisted." Dapper becomes further enmeshed in their conniving when he readily believes their story that he is related to the Queen of Fairy. To obtain her aid, however, Dapper must first "be bath'd and fumigated," fast, and put on a clean shirt, ritual activities highly suggestive of the white magician's preparatory ceremonies. Dapper willingly parts with twenty nobles when he learns that the Queen of Fairy "may hap to leaue" him "all she has."

The meeting proves to be ruinous. Blindfolded, his handkerchiefs, his rings, and his cash filched, he is pinched all over his body by the trio, who now masquerade as fairies. Yet Dapper remains a willing gull to the end. Even after an enforced imprisonment in the privy, he still promises

Dol, as the Queen of Fairy, large sums for the chance that she will leave him "three or foure hundred chests of trea-sure, and some twelue thousand acres of *Faeirie* land."

Another gull, Abel Drugger, tells Subtle that he was directed to the house by "one Captain Face, that says you know men's planets, and their good angels and their bad." Drugger wants astrological direction for the most auspicious ways to conduct business in his new tobacco shop, ways he believes he can come to know "by art" and "by *necromancie.*" This latter pursuit, raising spirits of the dead, is the black magician's sphere, an area this charlatan avoids.

In an instant, Subtle becomes a prophet. He predicts that Drugger will prosper, both in riches and in honors, become a member of his guild, and then achieve the status of an alderman. This forecast loosens Drugger's purse strings. At the same time, Subtle claims an ability to predict with "metoposcopie," the skill of judging character and fortune through diagnosis of features on the face and forehead:

> A certaine starre i' the fore-head, which you see not.
> Your chest-nut, or your oliue-colour'd face
> Do's neuer faile: and your long eare doth promise.
> I knew't, by certaine spots too, in his teeth,
> And on the naile of his mercurial finger.
>   (I, iii, 45–49)

This skill is undoubtedly the same as physiognomy, the province, we have seen, of Della Porta.

Moving rapidly, Subtle next employs the techniques of chiromancy, or the reading of the hand, throwing out the lure of astrological jargon to catch the impressionable Drugger:

> The thumbe, in *chiromancie,* we giue VENVS;
> The fore-finger to LOUE; the midst, to SATVRNE;
> The ring to SOL; the least, the MERCVRIE:
> Who was the lord, sir, of his *horoscope,*
> His *house of life* being Libra, which fore-shew'd,

He should be a merchant, and should trade with ballance.
                                        (I, i, 52–57)

Connecting the parts of the hand to the planets in fast succession, Subtle predicts the arrival of a ship filled with "a
commoditie of drugs" for the tobacconist. He then suggests
certain mercurial spirits whose names Drugger should paint
in specific locations within the shop. The charlatan's mention
of minerals leads him to forecast that Drugger will actually
produce the philosopher's stone itself. The prospect of so
rosy a future drives Drugger to yet more liberal spending
and a final request for "an *almanack*" in which Subtle will
mark down all his client's ill-omened astrological days. A
further consultation over a propitious sign for the tobacco
shop elicits Subtle's recommendation of spelling Drugger's
name "in some mystick character." Even the name of Dr.
Dee is called upon in the composition of this sign of *"mys-
terie* and *hieroglyphick."*

Drugger's final request is that Subtle and Face procure
for him the hand of Dame Pliant. This attempted soliciting
disintegrates into a private dispute between the two charlatans over their own rights to the lady in question. Yet none
of the schemers succeeds: Lovewit takes the widow and
gulls them all.

Of his most important client, Sir Epicure Mammon,
Subtle declares, "If his dreame last, he'll turne the age, to
gold," for Mammon talks "as he were possess'd" of owning
"the *stone,"* advocating all to *"be rich":*

> He will make
> Nature asham'd, of her long sleepe: when art
> Who's but a step-dame, shall doe more, then shee,
> In her best loue to man-kind, euer could.
>   (I, iv, 25–28)

In a swelling Marlovian rhetoric, Mammon eulogizes the
infinite Faust-like powers that he believes will be his as
future owner of the philosopher's stone and the elixir:

He that has once the *flower of the sunne,*
The perfect *ruby,* which we call *elixir,*

. . . .

Can confer honour, loue, respect, long life,
Giue safety, valure: year, and victorie,
To whom he will.

(II, i, 47–48, 50–52)

To support his dream, Mammon calls upon antiquity, no
less than "a treatise penn'd by ADAM" on the philosopher's
stone. He even vaunts ownership of a piece of Jason's gold-
en fleece, as the Pardoner might his relics in *The Canterbury
Tales.*

Jonson admirably plays off this unquestioning emotional
acceptance of white magic against the counterpoint of his
friend Surly's profound skepticism. To Mammon's prag-
matic friend, who "would not willingly be gull'd," the
evidence of magic is both shaky and dubious. "Your stone
canot transmute me," Surly states flatly. Significantly, being
put to the test in his presence, Subtle's performance comes
closest to that of a white magician. He is filled with piety
at prayer, "doing his deuotions, for the successe," and is
sharply contrasted to the fantastic, self-indulgent Mammon,
who claims his dreams will be fulfilled for him because he
is sponsoring the alchemy. Surly, apparently well acquainted
with the holy occupation of white magicians, is dubious of
Mammon's luxury:

Why, I haue heard, he must be *homo frugi,*
A pious, holy, and religious man,
One free from mortall sinne, a very virgin.

(II, ii, 97–99)

But the deluded Mammon does not recognize that Surly's
statement is directed at him—that he should be devout and
priestlike, not lustful and arrogant. As long as Subtle appears godly, that will be sufficient for Mammon:

That Makes it, sir, he is so. But I buy it.

My venter brings it me. He, honest wretch,
A notable, superstitious, good soule,
Has worne his knees bare, and his slippers bald,
With prayer, and fasting for it: and, sir, let him
Do it alone, for me, still.

                                    (II, ii, 100–105)

Mammon's plans are wildly grandiose, inflated with fantasies of temporal power and sexual voluptuousness.

To lure his victim into the trap, Subtle introduces himself to his two visitors as a hyper-pious man, warning them of the dangerous consequences of lustfully sullying the devout atmosphere that surrounds the experiment:

                                    I should be sorry,
To see my labours, now, e'ene at perfection,
Got by long watching, and large patience,
Not prosper, where my loue, and zeale hath plac'd 'hem.
Which (heauen I call to witnesse, with your selfe,
To whom, I have pour'd my thoughts) in all my ends,
Haue look'd no way, but vnto publique good,
To pious vses, and deere charitie,
Now growne a prodigie with men. Wherein
If you, my sonne, should so preuaricate,
And, to your owne particular lusts, employ
So great, and catholique a blisse: be sure,
A curse will follow, yea, and ouertake
Your subtle, and most secret wayes.

                                    (II, iii, 10–23)

The ensuing scene provides an interplay among three points of view: the white magician himself (even though he is feigned here), his unquestioning advocate, and his skeptical detractor. Undoubtedly the audience both believed and disbelieved the white magic represented by these figures.

Subtle and Face work their hardest to dislodge Surly's disbelief in the philosopher's stone and, as the alchemical experiment supposedly reaches its climax, Subtle puts Face through a series of professional paces that involve the purportedly crucial procedures of infusion and filtering. Surly likens these terms to canting, and at the mention of materials, amalgams, mercury, fixation, and the philosopher's vinegar, drily comments, "we shall have a salad."

Mammon impatiently seeks the climactic *"proiection,"* when all the metal articles he has brought to the house may be converted to gold. Although Subtle hedges, declaring how necessary it is to repeat the refining process several times, he urges Mammon to

> get you your stuff here, against after-noone,
> Your brasse, your pewter, and your andirons.
>
> (II, ii, 115–16)

Still refusing to be gulled, Surly indicts the profession and throws back Subtle's terminology to his face.

> . . . I'll beleeue,
> That *Alchemie* is a pretty kind of game,
> Somewhat like tricks o' the cards, to cheat a man,
> With charming. . . . What else are all your termes,
> Whereon no one o' your writers grees with other?
>
> (II, ii, 179–88)

To fend off this onslaught, Subtle claims the symbols are necessary for an art that writers have purposely obscured, citing examples of Egyptian hieroglyphics, scriptural parables, poetic fables, and allegories.

The momentary, accidental appearance of Dol abruptly breaks off this debate. Surly sees this as tangible proof: "Hart, this is a bawdy house! I'll be burnt else." Subtle's serene religious pose crumbles. Mammon rushes to Subtle's defense to describe him as

> an excellent *Paracelsan!* and has done
> Strange cures with *minerall physicke.* He deals all
> With *spirits* he. He will not hear a word
> Of GALEN, or his tedious recipe's.
>
> (II, iii, 230–33)

But Surly remains unconvinced, and Face, fearing that Surly's vindictive attack on white magic will deprive them of Mammon's money, manufactures an excuse to get Surly out of the house. Surly leaves, later to return, disguised as a Spanish Don who can speak no English. The avaricious charlatans openly reveal their duplicity before him, and are exposed by Surly for what they are: "a nest of villains!"

Dol meanwhile entices Mammon, and his triumphantly rhetorical wooing of her foretells a future of golden pleasures—on drinking the elixir, they will "enjoy a perpetuitie of life, and lust." But Subtle, reappearing as the pristine white magician, wonders that he "would so tempt heauen" with lust and thus lose his fortunes, for "this'll retard the *worke,* a month at least."

"A great crack and noise within" signals that all is lost. Face runs in:

> O sir, we are defeated! all the *workes*
> Art flown *in fumo:* euery glasse is burst.
> Fornace, and all rent doene! as if a bolt
> Of thunder had been driuen through the house.
> *Retorts, Receiuers, Pellicanes, Bolt-heads,*
> All strooke in shiuers!
>
> (IV, v, 57–62)

Mammon is devastated that nothing can be recovered, but accepts his lack of dedication as reason: "O my voluptuous mind! I am iustly punish'd." Repentence is recommended as the only medicine for "the curst fruits of vice, and lust."

As Dame Pliant and Kastril are only peripheral in our concern with white magic, the last two major characters of the play who are gulled by the feigned use of white magic are Ananias, a deacon, and Tribulation, a pastor. Both are Puritans from Amsterdam, in exile from their native England. Like Mammon, their interest is also in the philosopher's stone, even though Ananias sees it as "a worke of darknesse, and with *Philosophie,* blinds the eyes of man."

Yet, they reason, their desire to obtain money to convert everyone to their religion is not wrong, for it is in a holy cause. Their hypocritical pose of extreme holiness is contrasted with their pragmatism and dishonesty. They see the philosopher's stone as a means of support for "silenced saints"—that is, Puritan exiles like themselves—and they need *aurum potabile* to bribe English civil magistrates so that they may return to England. The metal that they are to bring to the house will be forged into Dutch dollars, an illegal kind of coining that Ananias calls casting and neatly justifies:

> The holy *Synode*
> Haue been in prayer, and meditation, for it.
> And 'tis reueal'd no lesse, to them, then me,
> That casting of money is most lawful.
> (IV, vii, 75–78)

However, the climactic explosion of the furnace destroys the wish-fulfillment dreams of the two Puritans as much as it has Mammon's; Subtle, now wishing to keep their money and be rid of them, urges the brethren to return to prayer and fasting to avoid incarceration in the Tower for tampering in alchemy.

The collapse of the alchemical enterprise, hastened by the return of Lovewit, signals the disintegration of the charlatans' venture. "I'll into mine old shape againe," declares Face, slipping into the role of Jeremy the butler once more. Symbolically, the metamorphoses are over, each of the trio assuming his original role, the alchemical mutations having come to naught. Once the deception is penetrated and no devout white magician is found to be at its center, the cries from the gulled are loud and long, for it is clear now that their hopes were baseless.

Within the concept of alchemy, the charlatans have indeed raised and inflated themselves, in a charade-like endeavor transmuting their roles from quack and whore to white

magician and Fairy Queen; yet, with the speculative undertaking shattered, they are reduced again to base vagabonds.
With mystical trappings shed from alchemy, Jonson reveals
it as a spur for man's devotion to money. This worship can
never transmute men, it being solely an obsessive, loveless
search for luxury and security. As the clients have also
raised themselves—through the fantasy of a glorious, prob-
lem-free future—so they, too, are confronted with their
grasping selves and no fulfillment. Indeed, the philosophers'
original vision of stone and elixir that could transform all
into a paradise, has attracted the worthless of the world
rather than the truly pious white magician-philosopher who
alone can achieve and control such a discovery.

The notion of a healing elixir, whose cure-all powers
supposedly fulfill every desire and sustain life indefinitely,
was the perfect idea for all those posing as healers. Its elu-
sive quality and beckoning promise was ideal for financial
gain. As Jonson employs alchemy, its ramifications become
multi-leveled, interchangeably overlapping in business, religion, and healing. The drive to discover gold is both
worship and commercial enterprise, as well as a key to
unlimited sexual prowess that will prolong man's happiness
forever. Yet it is on man himself that the pseudo-alchemists
parasitically feed. Their activity here underscores the future
trends of manipulative relationships in a growing age of
commerce.

Whether a force for good or for confusion, the characters
who—truly or falsely—put on the robes of the white magician usually fit the role of the "agent" in Elizabethan/
Jacobean plot structures. With mystical foreknowledge and
the power of a puppeteer, the true white magician—or his
more powerful counterpart, the mythological god or divinely
inspired king—could bring reconciliation, restitution, and
the benevolent reordering of society to the other characters.
On the other hand, with realistic insight and eager cunning,

the charlatan magician could, under the guise of doing good, manipulate his gulls and make fortunes, until he entangled himself in his own plot, or made a fatal error in judgment. But whether genuine or false, the aura of magic was an obvious source of dramatic excitement for the playwright, and, more important, it lent itself as an attribute to the various kinds of personal power that so many Renaissance plays explored. One source for the power figure itself— when a force for evil—can be traced to the Medieval drama, where the character of Vice would manipulate others very much as do agents like Iago, in his complex tragic world, and Subtle, in his complicated comic one. Similarly, from wellsprings as old as Aristophanes and Merlin, the figure of the older man with a powerful will to good becomes, in Shakespeare, embodied in such figures as the nonmagic-wielding Duke Vincentio, the quasi-magician Paulina at the end of *The Winter's Tale,* and the genuine white magician Prospero. Most important for us, the combination of the traditional agent figure with the Renaissance concepts of white magic produced on the English stage many theatrically effective moments in the drama of the time.

Selected Bibliography

Agrippa, Cornelius. *The Vanity of Arts and Sciences.* London, 1676.
———. *Three Books of Occult Philosophy.* Translated by J. F. London, 1651.
Allen, D. C. *Mysteriously Meant.* Baltimore, 1970.
———. *The Star-Crossed Renaissance.* Durham, N.C., 1941.
Anon. (John Day? John Lyly). *The Maydes Metamorphosis.* Edited by John S. Farmer. London, 1908.
———. (Arthur Munday?). *The Rare Triumphs of Love and Fortune.* Edited by W. W. Greg. Oxford, 1931.
Augustine. *The City of God.* Translated by Marcus Dods. New York, 1950.
Aristotle. *Metaphysica.* Translated by W. D. Ross. Oxford, 1908.
Bacon, Francis. *Works.* Edited by Spedding *et al.* 3 vols. London, 1857–1859.
Barish, Jonas A. *Ben Jonson and the Language of Prose Comedy.* Cambridge, 1960.
Baskervill, Charles, *et al,* eds. *Elizabethan and Stuart Plays.* New York, 1934.
Blau, Joseph Leon. *The Christian Interpretation of the Cabala in the Renaissance.* New York, 1944.
Bodin, Jean. *De la Demonamie des Sorciers.* Paris, 1580.
Briggs, K. M. *The Anatomy of Puck.* London, 1959.
———. *Pale Hecate's Team.* London, 1962.
Brown, Norman O. *Hermes the Thief.* Madison, Wis., 1947.

138

Browne, William. *Poems.* Edited by Gordon Goodwin, II. London, 1893.

Bruno, Giordano. *The Candlebearer* (1582). Translated by J. R. Hale, in Eric Bentley, ed., *The Genius of the Italian Theater.* New York, 1964.

Bultmann, Rudolph. *Primitive Christianity in its Contemporary Setting.* New York, 1956.

Butler, E. M. *The Myth of the Magus.* Cambridge, 1948.

———. *Ritual Magic.* Cambridge, 1949.

Campbell, Lily B. *Scenes and Machines on the English Stage.* Cambridge, 1923.

Campion, Thomas. *Poetical Works.* Edited by Percival Vivian. London, 1907.

Casaubon, Meric. *A True and Faithfull Relation of What passed for many years Between Dr. John Dee (A Mathematician of Great Fame in Q. Eliz. and King James their Reignes) and Some Spirits.* London, 1659.

Cassirer, Ernst. *The Individual and the Cosmos in Renaissance Philosophy.* Translated by Mario Domandi. New York, 1964.

Castiglioni, Arturo. *Adventures of the Mind.* New York, 1946.

Chambers, E. K. *The Elizabethan Stage.* 4 vols. Oxford, 1923.

Chaucer, Geoffrey. *Works.* Edited by F. N. Robinson. Cambridge, Mass., 1957.

Clubb, Louise George. *Giambattista Della Porta, Dramatist.* Princeton, 1965.

Cornford, F. M. *The Origin of Attic Comedy.* Edited by Theodor H. Gaster. New York, 1961.

Craig, Hardin. "Magic in *The Tempest." Philological Quarterly* 67: 8–15.

———. *The Enchanted Glass.* Oxford, 1960.

Culpeper, Nicholas. *The Complete Herbal.* London, 1653.

Cunningham, Dolora. "The Jonsonian Masque as a Literary Form," *ELH* 22 (1955): 108–24.

Cunningham, J. V. *Woe or Wonder: The Emotional Effect of Shakespearean Tragedy.* Denver, 1951.

Curry, Walter Clyde. *Shakespeare's Philosophical Patterns.* Baton Rouge, 1937.

Dalton, Michael. *The Countrey Justice.* London, 1677.

Davenant, William. *Works.* 2 vols. London, 1872.

Demaray, John G. *Comus as a Masque.* New York, 1967.

de Perrott, Joseph. *The Probable Source of the Plot of Shakespeare's Tempest.* Worcester, Mass., 1905.

Donne, John. *Works.* Edited by Alfull. London, 1839.

Doran, Madeleine. *Endeavors of Art.* Madison, Wis., 1964.

————. "On Elizabethan 'Credulity,' " *Journal of the History of Ideas* 1 (April, 1940) : 151–76.

Ellacombe, H. N. *The Plant-lore and Garden-craft of Shakespeare.* London, 1878.

Erasmus. *Ten Colloquies.* Translated by Craig R. Thompson. New York, 1957.

Evans, Herbert A., ed. *English Masques.* London, 1897.

Fell-Smith, Charlotte. *John Dee, 1527–1608.* London, 1909.

Frye, Northrop. *A Natural Perspective.* New York, 1965.

————. *The Anatomy of Criticism.* Princeton, 1957.

Furniss, W. Todd. "Ben Jonson's Masque," in *Three Studies in the Renaissance.* New Haven, 1958.

Greene, Robert. *Friar Bacon and Friar Bungay.* Edited by Daniel Seltzer. Lincoln, Neb., 1963.

The Grete Herball. London, 1526.

Halliwell, James Orchard, ed. *The Private Diary of Dr. John Dee.* London, 1842.

Harbage, Alfred. *Annals of English Drama (973–1700).* London, 1953.

Haydn, Hiram. *The Counter-Renaissance.* New York, 1960.

Hastings, James, ed. *A Dictionary of the Bible.* vol. 6, New York, 1902.

Hollander, John. *The Untuning of the Sky: Ideas of Music in English Poetry, 1500–1700.* Princeton, 1961.

Hooker, Richard. *Laws of Ecclesiastical Polity.* Edited by John Keble. London, 1888.

Hopper, Vincent Foster. *Medieval Number Symbolism.* New York, 1938.

Hunter, R. G. *Shakespeare and the Comedy of Forgiveness.* New York, 1965.

"I.C." (John Cumber?). *The Two Merry Milkmaids, or The Best Words Wear the Garland.* N.p., n.d.

James VI. *Daemonologie.* Edinburgh, 1597.

Jonas, Hans. *The Gnostic Religion.* Boston, 1958.

Jonson, Ben. *Works.* Edited by C. G. Simpson, Percy Simpson, and Evelyn Simpson. 11 vols. Oxford, 1925–1952.

Knight, G. Wilson. *The Shakespearean Tempest.* London, 1953.

Knights, L. C. *Drama and Society in the Age of Jonson.* London, 1937.

Koch, Kenneth. "The Physician in English Drama," M.A. thesis, Columbia University, 1953.

Koch, Rudolph. *The Book of Signs.* Translated by Vyvyan Holland. London, 1930.

Kocher, Paul H. *Science and Religion in Elizabethan England.* San Marino, Calif., 1953.

——. "The Witchcraft Basis in Marlowe's *Faustus,*" *MLN* 67 (1952) : 9.

Kristeller, Paul O. *Eight Philosophers of the Italian Renaissance.* Stanford, 1964.

——. "Renaissance Platonism," in *Facets of the Renaissance.* New York, 1963.

——. *The Philosophy of Marsilio Ficino.* Translated by Virginia Conant. Gloucester, Mass., 1964.

Langham, William. *The Garden of Health.* London, 1579.

Latham, Minor. *The Elizabethan Fairies.* New York, 1930.

Lea, K. M. *Italian Popular Comedy: a Study in the Commedia dell'Arte, 1560–1620, with Special Reference to the English Stage.* Oxford, 1934.

Leyel, C. F. *The Magic of Herbs.* London, 1932.

Lewis, C. S. *The Discarded Image.* Cambridge, 1964.

Lucian. *Selected Satires.* Translated and edited by Lionel Casson. New York, 1962.

Madsen, William. "The Idea of Nature in Milton's Poetry," in *Three Studies in the Renaissance.* New Haven, 1958.

McCarthy, J. R. *Rings Through the Ages.* New York, 1945.

Mersenne, Marin. *Questiones in Genesim.* Paris, 1625.

Milton, John. *Complete Poems and Major Prose.* Edited by Merritt Y. Hughes. New York, 1957.

Moyes, John. *Medicine and Kindred Arts in the Plays of Shakespeare.* Glasgow, 1896.

Munday, Anthony. *John A Kent and John A Cumber.* Edited by Muriel St. Clare Byrne. The Malone Society Reprints. Oxford, 1923.

Murry, John Middleton. *The Problem of Style.* London, 1939.

Nauert, Charles J. *Agrippa and the Crisis of Renaissance Thought.* 55 Illinois Studies in the Social Sciences. Urbana, 1965.

Nicoll, Allardyce. *Stuart Masques and the Renaissance Stage.* London, 1937.

Orgel, Stephen. *The Jonsonian Masque.* Cambridge, Mass., 1965.

Ovid. *The Metamorphoses.* Translated by William Golding, edited by W. H. D. Rouse. Carbondale, Ill., 1961.

Owst, Gerald. *Literature and Pulpit in Medieval England.* Cambridge, 1933.

Palmer, D. J. "Magic and Poetry in *Doctor Faustus.*" *Critical Quarterly* 6 : 56–67.

Paracelsus, Phillipus Aureolus. *Selected Writings.* Edited by Jolande Jacobi, translated by Norbert Guterman. New York, 1951.

Parr, Johnstone. *Tamburlaine's Malady.* University, Alabama, 1953.

Perkins, William. *A Discourse of the Damned Art of Witchcraft.* Cambridge, 1608.

———. *Works.* London, 1605.

Peter, John. *Complaint and Satire.* Oxford, 1956.

Philips, James E. "*The Tempest* and the Renaissance Idea of Man," SQ 15, no. 2 (1964) : 147–59.

Pico, "On the Dignity of Man." Translated by Elizabeth L. Forbes. *Journal of the History of Ideas* 3, no. 3 (June, 1942) : 352.

Prynne, William. *Histriomastix.* London, 1633.

Recorde, Robert. *The Pathway to Knowledge.* London, 1551.

Reed, Robert R. Jr. *The Occult on the Tudor and Stuart Stage.* Boston, 1965.

Reyher, Paul. *Les masques anglais.* Paris, 1909.

Rowley, William (& another?; 'William Shakespeare and William Rowley' on t.p.). *The Birth of Merlin,* Students' Facsimile Edition. N.p., n.d.

Scholem, Gershon G. *On the Kabbalah and its Symbolism.* Translated by Ralph Manheim. New York, 1965.

Scott, Mary A. *Elizabethan Translations after the Italian.* Boston, 1916.

Scoular, Kitty W. *Natural Magic: Studies in the Presentation of Nature in English Poetry from Spenser to Marvell.* Oxford, 1965.

The Secretes of the Reverend Maister Alexis, of Piemont. London, 1580.

Seligmann, Kurt. *The History of Magic*. New York, 1948.

Seznec, Jean. *The Survival of the Pagan Gods*. Translated by Barbara F. Sessions. New York, 1953.

Shakespeare, William. *The Tempest*. Edited by Frank Kermode. *Arden Shakespeare*, rev. ed. Cambridge, Mass., 1954.

Silhol, Robert. "Magie et utopie dans *La Tempête*." *Études Anglaises* 17 (1964) : 447–56.

Steele, Mary S. *Plays and Masques at Court*. New Haven, 1926.

Stillman, John Maxon. *The Story of Alchemy*. New York, 1960.

Strathmann, E. A. *Sir Walter Ralegh*. New York, 1951.

Tayler, Edward. *Nature and Art in Renaissance Literature*. New York, 1964.

Thorndike, Lynn. *A History of Magic and Experimental Science*. 8 vols. New York, 1923–1958.

————. *Magic in the Intellectual History of Europe*. New York, 1905.

Tomkis, Thomas. *Albumazar*. Edited by Hugh A. Dick, *University of California Publications in English* 13. Los Angeles, 1944.

Waite, A. E. *The Book of Ceremonial Magic*. New Hyde Park, 1961.

Walker, D. P. *Spiritual Magic from Ficino to Campanella*. London, 1959.

Walsh, J. J. *The Popes and Science*. London, 1912.

Welsford, Enid. *The Court Masque*. Cambridge, 1927.

West, R. H. *Shakespeare and the Outer Mystery*. Lexington, Kentucky, 1968.

————. *The Invisible World*. Athens, Ga., 1939.

Wilson, Harold S. "Action and Symbol in *Measure for Measure* and *The Tempest*," *SQ* 4 (1953) : 375–84.

Wind, Edgar. *Pagan Mysteries in the Renaissance*. New Haven, 1938.

Wright, Louis. *Middle-Class Culture in England*. Ithaca, 1935.

Wright, Thomas. *The Passions of the Mind*. London, 1604.

Yates, Frances. *Giordano Bruno and the Hermetic Tradition*. London, 1964.

Zimbardo, Rose Abdelnour. "Form and Disorder in *The Tempest*," *SQ* 14 (1963) : 49–56.

Index